TEN COLLOQUIES

The Library of Liberal Arts

TEN COLLOQUIES

ERASMUS

Translated, with introduction and notes, by
CRAIG R. THOMPSON

· ·

The Library of Liberal Arts
published by

Macmillan Publishing Company
New York
Collier Macmillan Publishers
London

nus: *c.* 1466-1536

Macmillan Publishing Company
866 Third Avenue
New York, New York, 10022
Collier Macmillan Canada, Inc.

PRINTING   20 21   YEAR   9 0 1 2 3 4 5
ISBN 0-02-420620-2

CONTENTS

. . . .

INTRODUCTION

I

In approaching the work of Erasmus, it may be better to keep before us the dates 1495-1536—those years in which virtually all his writings were produced—than to rely overmuch on conventional tags or generalizations about him and his epoch. Generalizations we must have, but they are more likely to be profitable if they develop from our reflections after we have read the texts than if they come to us ready-made. "Greatest humanist of the Renaissance," or some similar phrase, is the label usually attached to the name of Erasmus in encyclopedias or introductions. The label is correct but not precise. It is familiar; it tells us something at a glance, as a label should; but it begs the large, complex question of just what "Renaissance" and "humanist" mean. Try to define these words closely, and the difficulties quickly appear.

Fortunately, our reading of Erasmus or other sixteenth-century authors does not depend on agreement concerning the concept of "Renaissance" or the question of the relationship of the Renaissance to the Middle Ages. These are, of course, genuine and important problems, to which historians have found an impressive variety of solutions. There was a Renaissance, to be sure. We could argue that there have been many renaissances, in different lands, different ages, different activities. "Humanism" is equally ambiguous in common usage. It identifies modes of thought and art and education, yet some so-called humanistic doctrines are irreconcilable with others described by the same word. "Human," "humanistic," "humane," "humanitarian" all have distinctive meanings of their own in addition to common basic meanings. Erasmus the humanist was a Christian supernaturalist; but in certain modern writings on religion we often find "humanism" contrasted with "supernaturalism," as though the phrase "Christian humanist" were a contradiction in terms. Yet "Christian humanist" (why not "humanist Christian"?) continues to be used as a stock term in books about the Renaissance. "The" Renaissance? Even if we were to settle on "the" Renaissance and agree on the date of its occurrence, we should have to decide whether we meant renaissance generally (whatever that would be) or a renaissance in painting, literature, music, science, or some other department of human culture. We should discover that although there is sense in talking about "a renaissance" or "the Renaissance" in one field of activity, for example in Italian painting during a certain period, we must qualify the word "Renaissance" or readjust it as we move on to, say, seventeenth-century English poetry. Milton the Puritan was a Renaissance writer. So were Aretino, Calvin, Rabelais, Leonardo, More, Donne, Loyola. How much have they in common except that they all wrote in the sixteenth or seventeenth century?

Whatever the answer to this question, we may be sure that the more we investigated the history of the terms "Renaissance" and "humanism" or "humanist," the more complicated we should find them. Like "medieval," like that irrepressible pair "classical" and "romantic," the words "Renaissance" and "humanism" have both historical and critical associations, and as a result they bear so many meanings that indiscriminate use of the terms may confuse rather than clarify thought. Any attempt to use them consistently would undoubtedly compel us to make distinctions between other renaissances and "the" Renaissance in an art or a branch of learning or a region, and between "the" Renaissance in one century and "the" Renaissance in other centuries.

This much by way of caution only, not of prohibition, for labels so well established are unlikely to be discarded; nor need they be shunned if they are used with proper care. Erasmus himself used the concepts of "Renaissance" and "humanities" or "humane letters," although his terms for them did not always have the same reference that comparable terms have in modern English. To him, as to some other writers of the fifteenth and sixteenth centuries, "Renaissance" denoted first of all the recovery of sound (classical, they believed) Latin style, of literature and literary taste, after a long night of barbarism; that is, after the period that recent centuries have been pleased to look upon as the "Dark Ages" or "Middle Ages." Now this kind of Renaissance—which Erasmus, writing in 1518, dates from "about eighty years ago" [1]—extended to certain other arts and studies also,[2] yet the basis of it all was philological. The revival of philology opened the door to a new and improved understanding of ancient texts, sacred and secular. Philology, plus printing, made textual and historical criticism possible.[3] Better understanding and teaching of sacred and patristic texts could lead to what, in the judgment of Erasmus, would be the greatest blessing of all those offered by the "Renaissance": the restoration of biblical theology, a theology liberated from Scholastic accretions and centered once more on what he constantly calls "the sources." [4]

[1] *Erasmi Epistolae*, III, 384. 5.

[2] *Ibid.*, III, 384-385.

[3] "It has been said of Erasmus that he propounded the problem of criticism, but did little himself to solve it; and it must be confessed that this latter part is true enough. But his failings were the failings of his time—an age when archaeology and palaeography were in their cradles, and when textual criticism knew only the boldest and most dashing methods. His merit was to perceive that the invention of printing had brought in a new era of critical study, when a text once well and truly fashioned to embody the sum of existing knowledge could become a tool for hundreds of scholars, identical and invariable, on which each could rely, knowing that his friend was using precisely the same; also a standard by which new-found manuscripts could be tested. And thus the quest of critical accuracy moved at one bound to a higher plane" (P. S. Allen, *Erasmus: Lectures and Wayfaring Sketches*, 1934, pp. 4-5).

[4] "Ego studiis meis nihil aliud conatus sum quam ut bonas litteras paene sepultas apud nostrates excitarem; deinde ut mundum plus satis tribuentem Iudaicis ceremoniis ad verae et Evangelicae pietatis studium expergefacerem; postremo ut studia theologiae scholastica, nimium prolapsa ad inanium quaestiuncularum argutias, ad divinae Scripturae fontes revocarem" (*Erasmi Epistolae*, IV, 439. 35-40).

II

These pages serve to introduce a selection from one of Erasmus' books, his *Colloquia Familiaria* or "Informal Conversations," not to present a sketch of his career. Curiosity about an author is more often the result of reading his books than an inducement to read them. Anyone curious about Erasmus or his place in history will find plenty of biographies and special studies to enlighten him. Nevertheless there may be excuse for saying something here about his early life, since a summary of it will take us as far as his Paris years, when the history of the *Colloquies* begins.[5]

Erasmus was born in 1466 or thereabouts (he himself gives different dates, and he had a bad memory for figures) at Gouda, near Rotterdam, or at Rotterdam itself. His father, whose name was probably Rogerius Gerardus, was a priest, though whether he had been ordained at the time of Erasmus' birth is uncertain; his mother was a widow named Margaret.[6] Erasmus was their second son.

He attended school for a few years at Gouda, then went as a chorister to the cathedral school at Utrecht, and after that to St. Lebwin's school at Deventer, where some of his teachers

[5] We have many valuable sources of information about the life of Erasmus, for he was famous in the world of literature and scholarship, lived in many different places, and kept up friendships with many distinguished persons. The best sources are a long letter by Erasmus to a secretary at the papal court, 1516 (*Erasmi Epistolae*, II, 291-312); a short autobiography, the *Compendium Vitae*, 1524 (*ibid.*, I, 47-52; its authenticity is not accepted by all scholars); two memoirs by a friend (*ibid.*, I, 52-71); and Erasmus' correspondence. He was one of the great letter writers, and if nothing else survived from his pen, his letters alone would assure him a permanent place in the literary history of his age. We do not accept a man's letters as unbiased autobiography, but when we check Erasmus' statements about himself in letters with what we learn from other sources, we can elicit a great deal of reliable information about him.

[6] Charles Reade's once-famous novel, *The Cloister and the Hearth*, an imaginative retelling of Gerard's life, borrows many scenes and incidents from the *Colloquies* and other writings of Erasmus.

were Brethren of the Common Life. This was a lay order, founded by Gerard Groote, a native of Deventer, in the late fourteenth century. Its members were not bound by irrevocable vows, but they had high ideals of poverty, practiced a common devotional life, and were celebrated for their piety and humility. They had little use for what they considered the unprofitable subtleties of metaphysics or the excessive ambitions of formal theological systems. (*The Imitation of Christ*, by one of the Brethren, probably Thomas à Kempis, is the greatest literary expression of their spirit.) A comparable emphasis on simple piety and on the ethical demands of the gospel, along with a distaste for the pretensions of Scholastic philosophy, is recurrent in the writings of Erasmus. In basic conceptions of Christianity there is a significant affinity between his habitual outlook and that of the Brethren of the Common Life. He was a dedicated scholar who spent his life advancing what he called "good learning," but he did not believe that finite, human learning could pluck the heart out of the mystery of existence or "by searching find out God." Appreciation of the harmony of learning and religion, reason and revelation, postulated in Erasmian thought is a key to understanding the man and his ideas.

After Erasmus and his brother Peter had been at Deventer nine years (1475-1484), an outbreak of plague forced them to return home. Their mother had died of the plague in 1483; their father died in 1484. The guardians who took charge of the boys put them in a school at Hertogenbosch for several years, then urged them (as they had done earlier) to become monks. Peter went first, Erasmus later and evidently with some reluctance. He entered (about 1487) the priory of Augustinian Regulars at Steyn, near Gouda, and there spent six years. At the end of a year he made his profession; five years later he was ordained priest. He had no true vocation for the monastic life, a fact that colors some of his later pronouncements on monasticism.

An appointment as Latin secretary to the Bishop of Cambrai (between 1492 and 1494) gave him a chance to leave the

priory. A few years later (1495) he went to the University of
Paris. Like many other intelligent students, then and now, he
had plenty of fault to find with collegiate life, the curriculum,
and the professors. (His longest colloquy, "A Fish Diet," includes a satirical passage on the College of Montaigu, where he
lived.) The lectures he thought intolerably dull—he was supposed to be studying for a degree in divinity—but he settled
down to considerable work of his own, coached pupils, made
friends with scholars, broke into print; in short, began to
establish himself in a modest way as a man of letters. He had
no intention of returning to Steyn. For many years, however,
he remained uneasy about his status (he abandoned his Augustinian costume in 1506), and at times he feared that ecclesiastical superiors might try to force him to go back to the
priory. Finally (1516) he obtained a papal dispensation per-
mitting him to live in the world. In effect, this dispensation
promised him freedom of action for the rest of his life.

From 1499, when he made a visit to England, until his death
in 1536, the chronicle is so full that it could not easily be
reduced to a few paragraphs: how he lived in Italy (1506-
1509) and in England (his last visit was in 1517), where he
became the close friend of Colet, More, and many other
eminent persons, taught Greek for a time at Cambridge,
and was honored by the Court and by churchmen; became
the leading figure in the literary and scholarly world of
his day; was appointed to the Council (a nominal post) of
Prince Charles of Spain, the future Emperor Charles V; lived
in Antwerp, Louvain, Basel, Freiburg im Breisgau; studied
incessantly, corresponded with his friends, engaged in controversies, wrote and edited books year after year. These are
only a few exterior facts. They are not spectacular; he did
nothing dramatic. But he had the dramatist's eye; he saw
everything, and had a remarkable gift for re-creating scenes
with his pen. His charming, witty letters and his entertaining
sketches of men and manners enable us to know the earlier
sixteenth century as well as we can now hope to know it
through a single witness.

To infer that he wanted only to exhibit that world, or to record its ways for the sake of amusement, would be a serious error. He wanted to instruct it. But the writings by which he is best known to most modern readers are not those which he himself regarded as the most instructive or significant ones. He set more store by many others of his books than his *Colloquies.* In one colloquy, "Cyclops," a character who is enumerating the calamities of the times says: "Kings make war, priests are zealous to increase their wealth, theologians invent syllogisms, monks roam through the world, the commons riot, Erasmus writes colloquies." The ironic anticlimax of this sentence is typical of the depreciatory tone Erasmus sometimes adopted in referring to his dialogues. On certain occasions he took them very seriously, as did his critics; on others, especially when it was advantageous to do so, he dismissed them as minor, lighter compositions. Probably both attitudes were sincere, despite apparent inconsistency. The attention he gave to the steadily expanding volume of colloquies, his concern for its reputation, and the trouble he took to defend it against attack are sufficient proof of his sensitivity about the book. On the other hand, if we examine his repeated affirmations of purpose as a writer, we can understand why the *Colloquies* could not, in his estimation, be counted among his most important works. He became fond of these dialogues; he came to take them far more seriously than he had at first; but many of them were essentially diversions, to be classed, like the *Praise of Folly,* among the writings described by his best editor as "trifles which he threw off to amuse himself, and of which he never ventured to be proud." [7] Could he have foreseen the day when, of all his books, only the *Praise of Folly* and the *Colloquies* would still be widely known, and his learned commentaries and editions scarcely opened except by scholars, he might have revised some particular literary judgments, but assuredly he would not have changed his mind about the relative importance of his biblical or patristic labors and his *belles lettres.*

[7] P. S. Allen, *Erasmus: Lectures and Wayfaring Sketches* (1934), p. 1.

That Erasmus could change his mind from time to time regarding the *Colloquies* need not surprise us, then, provided we remember the main purpose of his lifework. This purpose was the advancement of learning and of the Christian religion. It was by his efforts in this direction that he wished to be judged. It was to this end that he produced, with prodigious toil, dozens of books, some of which remained useful to men for many generations: editions of the Fathers of the Church (Jerome, Cyprian, Hilary, Irenaeus, Ambrose, Augustine, Origen); editions and paraphrases of the Greek New Testament; commentaries and homilies; moral, religious, and political essays (e.g., *Enchiridion, Ratio Verae Theologiae, Paraclesis, Modus Orandi Deum, Christiani Matrimonii Institutio, De Praeparatione ad Mortem, Ecclesiastes, Institutio Principis Christiani, Querela Pacis,* to name only some of the best-known ones); works on education (*De Ratione Studii, De Copia, De Civilitate*); editions and translations of classical authors; a huge dictionary of proverbs, the *Adagia*.

These, like everything else Erasmus wrote, were in Latin, the international language of educated men. Latin was the best way, indeed the only way, of reaching the readers he most desired to influence. He assumed, as did his public, that Latin should be the basis of education.[8] For to understand the world, we must understand the past. And this obviously requires knowledge of the enduring human achievements in art, literature, law, philosophy. Since so many of these achievements were Greek and Roman, we must study Greek and Roman civilization; which means that first we must learn their languages. "Almost everything worth knowing has been set forth in these two tongues." [9]

[8] One of the seventeenth-century editions of the *Colloquies*, that by Peter Rabus, is dedicated to the editor's seven-year-old son, who, we surmise, was expected to handle the Latin, although the father was generous enough to help him with the occasional Greek and Hebrew phrases.

[9] *Erasmi Opera Omnia* (Leiden edition), I, 521B.

III

Deeply involved in the intellectual and religious conflicts of his time, Erasmus did not, and could not, lead men through the force of his personality or by the example of heroic actions. As he himself confessed, he lacked the hero's or martyr's courage.[10] He was not a Luther or a Loyola. Nor had he, as his friend More had, firsthand experience in political administration and responsibility. His office was that of the thinker and writer whose opportunity of influencing mankind lies in his gift of eloquence or lucidity, who seems to express so well a point of view, a set of presuppositions, an ideology that his writings become identified with, or symbolize, a profound interpretation of events or ideas. How much effect his books had on social and religious thought is quite debatable, but there is no question that, taken as a whole, they furnish the best example of one significant type of thought in the sixteenth century: the complex of assumptions and beliefs indicated by the common, if questioned, label "Christian humanism." Its inspiration was Christian and classical. The ideas themselves were not new, but they were communicated in a style and idiom that distinguished them from the Christian, moralistic, and "humanistic" expression of earlier periods. This "Christian humanism," then, governs Erasmus' concepts of religion and ethics (and accounts for his tendency to depreciate metaphysics), his notion of education as a training based on the classics, and his social criticism—for example, in his tractates on war, which were often reprinted.

His later years were distressed by the widening schism in the Church. When viewed in perspective, the Reformation may seem, in Whitehead's phrase, "a domestic affair of the European races," but without careful study of the Reformation any effort to comprehend sixteenth-century civilization would be futile. Similarly we must try to understand the re-

[10] *Erasmi Epistolae,* IV, 541. 26-34.

actions of Erasmus to the Reformation if we are to make sense
of his later writings and their relation to his society.

When Luther came onto the scene in 1517-1518, Erasmus
was a literary celebrity and a biblical and patristic scholar of
international fame. His writings on religion, principally *Enchiridion* and the prefaces to the Greek New Testament, had
familiarized readers in many lands with his strictures on abuses
in the Church and his summons to a simpler, purer Christianity, purged of formalism and superstition, more concerned
with recapturing the spirit of the primitive Church than with
ceremonialism and hierarchy. After the emergence of Lutheranism, whatever he wrote on religion or the customs of the
Church was sure to be closely scrutinized by his readers, not
least by those already hostile to him. His position was a difficult one. In a society habitually intolerant on principle in
matters of religion, he advocated a measure of toleration. In
the quarrels over Luther—for whom, at first, he had many
good words—he tried to moderate differences, hoping that a
compromise could be reached and schism avoided.[11] Events
shattered his hopes. Suspected, rightly or wrongly, of attempt-
ing to stay above the battle while presuming to pass judgment
on both sides, he found himself drawn closer and closer to the
conflict, until he was forced at last to abandon any pretense
of neutrality.

Not that he was ever neutral on the question of his loyalty
to the Roman Church. However severe his criticism of many
aspects of ecclesiastical life and government, he never thought
of leaving the Church or of aligning himself with the Lutherans; nor did he think that weakness or corruption in the
visible Church justified secession from it. Reform was desperately needed, he believed, but he wanted it to come from
within the Church. This position often caused him to be mis-
understood. Many readers insisted on identifying his criticism
with Luther's, a natural if superficial judgment. Luther himself distrusted Erasmus from the first. But Erasmus' enemies

[11] His early opinions on Luther and Lutheranism are reviewed in my
edition of the colloquy *Inquisitio de Fide* (1950), pp. 1-49.

took pleasure in taunting him with charges of Lutheran sympathies. "Aut Erasmus Lutherissat, aut Erasmissat Lutherus," as one Spanish detractor put it.[12]

Erasmus agreed emphatically that many of the abuses assailed by Luther needed to be attacked. Indeed, he himself had been attacking them for years before Luther was heard of. He was quick to recognize the power of Luther's writings, to sense their appeal to Luther's countrymen, and he was impatient with the obstinacy of some of Luther's opponents. On the other hand, he was repelled by what he considered the intransigence and turbulence of the Lutherans, whom he blamed for stirring up civil strife. Yet he warned Pope Adrian VI that attempts to suppress them by force would prove difficult and mistaken. Such a policy had failed to stamp out the Wycliffites in England.[13] His own efforts to stay free of direct engagement in the controversies finally yielded to the insistence of the orthodox that he write against Luther. This he did, not by attacking Luther personally but by publishing a treatise (*De Libero Arbitrio*, 1524) in which he opposed the Lutheran doctrine of the will—that central issue in Lutheran teaching, as Luther himself acknowledged in his reply (*De Servo Arbitrio*, 1525).

Erasmus' letters of 1518-1524 reveal how anxiously he kept track of Lutheran affairs. A few years later he was to witness at close range the activities of Zwingli's followers in Basel. As time passed, his opinions on Lutherans hardened, yet he could never convince some of his own opponents in the Roman Church that he was free from Lutheran sympathies. To them he seemed but a proud, indifferent, unfilial son of the Church; a brilliant writer perhaps, but a disingenuous and superficial thinker on religion, whose literary reputation could neither conceal nor palliate the mischievousness of his writings.

When we read his amusing dramatic sketches of unlettered or hypocritical monks and friars, unworthy pastors, or worldly prelates, we are not to assume that he was an unprejudiced

[12] *Erasmi Opera Omnia* (Leiden edition), IX, 708A.
[13] *Erasmi Epistolae*, V, 260. 147–261. 169.

reporter or always a reliable witness. (Remember, too, that he wrote about good churchmen as well as bad ones.) He had profoundly serious arguments, from reasoned principles, to offer when writing on monasticism, ceremonies, biblical criticism, Scholastic philosophy, and other topics; but he had an emotional bias also—for example, on the subject of monasticism. Whether his experiences as a young man in the priory of Steyn were as unhappy as he implied afterwards, and whether, if they were, this was in part his own fault, is beside the point. Whatever the truth about his private experiences or inner life—and we may be sure he never tells us the whole story—his feelings on his favorite subjects were too strong, his dramatic instinct too dominant, to permit him to write about them dispassionately.

IV

Few great books had more modest beginnings than the *Colloquies*. The earliest parts date from the closing years of the fifteenth century, when Erasmus was living in Paris. There he helped to support himself by tutoring. He prepared for his pupils some simple exercises designed to teach correct conversational and written Latin. These phrases and sentences, many of them in dialogue form, are the oldest material in our collection of *Colloquies*. They are of this sort:

Christian. I thank you. I commend you. So I invite you to dinner tomorrow. I beg you, then, to dine with me tomorrow. So I beg you to have lunch with me tomorrow. So I want you for my guest tomorrow.

Augustine. But I fear I won't be free. I'm afraid I can't. I'll come if I'm free. But I'm afraid I won't be able to.

Christian. Why won't you be free? How come? Why so? What's the reason? On what ground? What cause? What's to hinder you? . . .

Augustine. I can't promise. I can't assure you of it. I'm unable to promise for certain. I'll come when it's most convenient for both of us.

Christian. Then I wish you'd name the day on which you'll dine with me. Then you'll have to name the day. Then you must promise a day.

Augustine. I wouldn't want you to know in advance. I don't want you to know in advance. I'll take you by surprise. . . .[14]

We cannot attach an exact date to these paragraphs; 1497 or 1498 is as close as we can come.[15] We can be fairly sure, however, of the names of the interlocutors. "Christian" is Christian Northoff of Lübeck; "Augustine," Augustine Vincent (known as Caminadus), who deserves a niche in literary history because it is due to his initiative that a book of Erasmus' *Colloquies* exists.

These "five-finger" exercises, useful pedagogically, no doubt, but of little or no literary value, were never intended for publication. Erasmus did not even keep a copy of them, he says.[16] But Augustine Vincent did save or obtain a copy. To it he added some scraps from other writings by Erasmus, and from Erasmus' letters. At some time, and by some means, this miscellany came into the hands of Lambert Hollonius of Liège, who in turn disposed of it to Beatus Rhenanus,[17] then an editor for Froben the printer, in Basel. It was printed and published by Froben, appearing in November, 1518, with the title *Familiarium Colloquiorum Formulae* and a preface by Beatus Rhenanus. Within a few months it was reprinted in Paris and Antwerp. Froben himself reprinted it, with a few pages of new material added, in February, 1519. Other reprints, either of the November, 1518, or the February, 1519, edition appeared during 1519 in Antwerp, Leipzig, Vienna, and Cracow. Meanwhile Erasmus, who had been surprised and annoyed by publication of the November, 1518, *Formulae,*

---

14 Translated from the Strasbourg text of May, 1519, pp. 16-17.

15 *Erasmi Epistolae,* I, 304. 92 n.; III, 465. 8.

16 *Ibid.,* XI, 287. 11.

17 One of the most eminent of Renaissance scholars. He became a close friend of Erasmus, and was his first biographer.

had the thin volume reissued, with some corrections and a preface by himself,[18] in March, 1519, at Louvain.

Other reprints, too, came out; but not until 1522 were large or significant additions made to the text. In that year Froben brought out two editions. The book became twice as long as the first edition, and much more than twice as interesting. (One of the colloquies translated in the present volume, "The Godly Feast," was a 1522 addition.) It was dedicated to the author's godson, Erasmius Froben (son of the printer), who is a speaker in one of the colloquies.

Between 1522 and 1533 twelve new, expanded editions of the book were published. At least one hundred reprintings of the various editions were made before Erasmus' death in 1536, a remarkable record in eighteen years. All in all, it was an enormously successful publication, hard to equal in the sixteenth century, perhaps. The final edition (1533) contained some fifty colloquies.[19] In addition, the rather long dialogue called *Ciceronianus* (1528), a work of considerable importance in the history of sixteenth-century literary criticism, was included in some editions of the *Colloquies* in Erasmus' lifetime. Later it was printed separately.

Naturally a book that went through so many editions and reprintings presents a rather complicated textual and bibliographical history. This is not the place for discussion of that history.[20] Be it enough to say that Erasmus made a good many changes in some editions. Other persons made unauthorized changes.

As a writer of international renown long before 1518, Erasmus had reason to be displeased by the unexpected appear-

[18] The text of this preface is reprinted in *Erasmi Epistolae,* III, 464-466.

[19] The total number is counted differently by different scholars, for it depends on how "colloquy" is defined. Many of the earlier pages consist of formulas of conversation rather than developed dialogues. There are at least fifty dialogues with separate titles deserving the name of colloquies.

[20] The nearest thing to a systematic account is that in the *Bibliotheca Erasmiana* (see bibliography at the end of this Introduction), supplemented by the notes in *Erasmi Epistolae.*

ance of the little book Beatus Rhenanus saw through the press. At first he did no more than permit it to be reprinted with corrections and a new preface. Busy with other projects, he probably gave little thought to what else could be made of such material. But in the editions of 1522 the *Colloquies* became a different book. By that date, or certainly by the next year, he had realized how much more might be done with a book of dialogues. At all events, there is no sign of his having conceived the idea of the *Colloquies*—as we know the book—earlier than 1521, and possibly we should put the date as late as 1523, for the edition of August, 1523, had ten new colloquies, including some of the best. (Translations of three of these, "The Shipwreck," "The Wooer and the Maiden," and "Inns," are included in this volume.)

What the 1522 and 1523 editions made clear was that colloquies offered Erasmus an admirable medium for expressing, freely but informally, his observations on current issues, institutions, ideas, customs, and even individuals. The ten dialogues selected for translation in this book are typical Erasmian treatments of favorite topics, but the variety in the collection is greater than this group shows. Debates on moral and religious questions; lively arguments on war, government, and other social problems; advice on how to train wives, husbands, or children; discussion of innkeepers, beggars, and horse thieves, of methods of study or of sleep, of diet, funerals, and sermons; literary criticism; even a colloquy composed of puns—all this and much more is in the complete *Colloquies*. Dialogue was one of the oldest of literary modes in prose, to be sure, and in the sixteenth century one of the most popular, but nowhere in that period do we find it used with more brilliance or more assurance than in Erasmus' book. The *Colloquies* were journalism of a sort, but many of them journalism so superior, so artistic, so far from ephemeral that they became literature. Those added from 1522 on had plot and structure; some had impressive characterization as well. They were incipient dramas or novelettes. As such, they may have contributed more than we suspect to the development of drama and prose fiction during the sixteenth and seventeenth centuries.[21]

Not all the colloquies are equally readable nowadays. Nor should we expect them to be, for in any large collection of writings there are bound to be inequalities. What matters is the large number of colloquies that can still give pleasure, still make the sixteenth century vivid to us. For all their six-teenth-century character and setting, these are no more out of date than the books of Rabelais or Cervantes. Sir Walter Raleigh's odd definition of great literature as that body of books which has been found useful in circumstances never contemplated by their authors [22] fits the *Colloquies* neatly. True, they may have to be read in a different key as well as a different tongue. And they can be read profitably for purposes never considered by their sixteenth-century public; for in-stance, as an introduction to the social and intellectual en-vironment of the sixteenth century itself. They take us by an-other route, through a different medium, into the milieu made familiar to us by Brueghel the Elder, Holbein the Younger, and Dürer, whose pictures are the best companions to the *Colloquies* a reader could wish.

To their author's natural dramatic talent were joined the moral purpose of a satirist and the temper of an ironist. Style is the man, we often hear. This man was shrewd, ironic, un-commonly observant, witty; at times able to suffer fools gladly. The irony was ingrained, a part of his character. We find it operative both in his serious and in his lighter works, but controlled by theme and purpose. In one composition, the *Praise of Folly*, it does more than affect the meaning. There theme and tone blend: the irony *becomes* the meaning. In the *Colloquies* irony is less pervasive and less profound, but still very important.

Less evident to some readers, but of interest to students of his thought, is the fact that the *Colloquies* often present in

[21] On their connection with the early novel see G. Saintsbury, *The Earlier Renaissance* (1923), pp. 81-84.

[22] G. S. Gordon, *The Discipline of Letters* (1946), p. 10.

dramatic, informal dress the ideas Erasmus had already published, or was later to publish, in his more formal writings.
Thus it is wise to check his essays and even commentaries
against colloquies on the same or related themes. If we find
that he writes an *ars moriendi* (*De Praeparatione ad Mortem*,
1534), we shall do well to compare it with what he wrote on
death and dying in the colloquy "The Funeral" (translated
in this volume) eight or nine years earlier. Half a dozen colloquies in the 1523 and the March, 1529, editions comprise a
"marriage group" illustrating pointedly and entertainingly
many of the admonitions set forth—with the customary posi-
tiveness of a moralist who is also a bachelor—in *Christiani
Matrimonii Institutio* (1526). After reading "Charon" (1529),
turn back to *Institutio Principis Christiani* (1516) and the famous *Querela Pacis* (1517). To understand better the position
of Erasmus in the controversies over Luther and Lutheranism,
read not only *De Libero Arbitrio* of September, 1524, but the
little-known colloquy *Inquisitio de Fide* of March, 1524.

V

In appraising the *Colloquies* we have to remember that although this was a book which began as one thing and became
something more, it did not forfeit its original purpose. It began as a school text, a short book of formulas, question-and-
answer sentences, brief paragraphs of statement. Then it was
enlarged; the dialogues grew longer, had plots, and could be
read for their own sakes as much as for correct Latin forms.
"It is the darling and delight of those who cultivate the
Muses," Erasmus allowed himself to boast when dedicating
the edition of August-September, 1524, to little Erasmius
Froben. "This book makes better Latinists and better persons." It provided practice in learning Latin by the time-
honored method of varying a phrase or sentence in order to
show what different ways there are of expressing a meaning,
and what the shades of difference signify. Like all successful

texts, it made the examples relevant to the pupils' interests.
It taught them how to express themselves *Latine* on matters
of home, friends, parents, games, school, holidays, and the like.

The book "caught on" from the first. It became a standard
textbook for schools, and continued to be used for three centuries. It was not the only book of Latin dialogues for schools,
of course, nor the only popular one, but it outlasted its com-
petitors; even in our own century one of the great university
presses published adaptations of it for beginners in Latin.[23]
To many persons it must have been the book most commonly
associated with the name of Erasmus, far better known than
his formal tractates on education.[24] We find it studied and
imitated; we even hear of colloquies being acted out by pupils.[25] To trace its fortunes in schools would require a survey
of humanistic education for several centuries, and in the New
World as well as the Old. The *Colloquies* came to America
with the Puritans. Every Harvard student in the seventeenth
century, we are told, "must have been familiar with the Colloquies of Erasmus," [26] a familiarity gained, no doubt, in
school rather than in college. A report on learning from modern Harvard gravely recommends putting "Renaissance Europe on the screen with the aid of Erasmus' *Colloquies*" as an
"immense educational eye opener." [27] If this could be done
without artistic damage to them, the *Colloquies* might prove
as helpful in the teaching of history as they once were in
linguistic and rhetorical training.

[23] *Colloquia Latina* and *Altera Colloquia Latina*, ed. G. M. Edwards
(Cambridge, Eng., 1906, 1908).

[24] Such as *De Ratione Studii* (1511); *De Copia* (1512); *De Recta Pro-
nuntiatione* (1528); *De Pueris Statim ac Liberaliter Instituendis* (1529).
Ciceronianus (1528) might be included, too. For a summary of Erasmus'
views on education see W. H. Woodward, *Desiderius Erasmus Concerning
the Aim and Method of Education* (1904).

[25] *Erasmi Epistolae*, VII, 508. 4 n.

[26] S. E. Morison, *Harvard College in the Seventeenth Century* (1936), p.
178; *The Puritan Pronaos* (1936), pp. 101-107. On Erasmus and Puritan-
ism see also Perry Miller, *The New England Mind: the Seventeenth Century* (1939), pp. 66, 90, 308, 339.

[27] *General Education in a Free Society* (1945), p. 264.

A student of literary history will notice in the *Colloquies* dozens of scenes or passages reminding him of themes, situations, and dialogues in vernacular literatures. Many a writer who had read the book, whether in school or out, must have remembered it. We know that Rabelais borrowed freely from it. Jonson knew it. Scott and Reade used whole colloquies for scenes in historical novels.[28] It would be pleasant to be able to affirm that Shakespeare read and used it. We have no absolute proof that he did so, but there are a few phrases and lines in the plays that very probably came from Erasmus' book.[29] Shakespeare's acquaintance with so popular a book is much more likely than unlikely.

The indebtedness of later writers to the *Colloquies* is a subject that deserves more attention than it has received. A comprehensive, critical account would not be easy to write. To list the obvious borrowings would be simple enough; to demonstrate indebtedness more subtle or elusive, though equally important, would not. Nevertheless the circulation of the *Colloquies,* and the impression we know it made on some sixteenth-century and later writers, justify us in thinking that there is much more to be found out and recorded about its influence on literature.

It was not popular with all readers. On the contrary, it was harshly condemned in some quarters. From the appearance of the 1522 editions until his death, Erasmus was compelled to defend it many times. He could—and did—protest that his too literal-minded opponents lost sight of the fact that sentiments expressed in a dialogue are those appropriate to the characters and to the dramatic situations, and are not necessarily the author's opinions. This was a perfectly plain, proper, and at times sincere defense. But it did not convince his stubborn critics, who suspected mere evasiveness in such replies.

Critics of the *Colloquies* made two major complaints. The

---

28 See headnotes to "The Shipwreck" and "Inns," pp. 3, 14.

29 For the evidence see T. W. Baldwin, *William Shakspere's Small Latine and Lesse Greeke* (1944), I, 735-744; J. A. K. Thompson, *Shakespeare and the Classics* (1952), pp. 71, 72-73, 96-97, 118, 126, 154.

first alleged that certain passages were indecent. This charge was not altogether surprising, for the book has a few passages that would probably be regarded as offensively coarse or as obscene by some readers today, as they were by some earlier readers. Erasmus attempted to brush the charge aside by retorting that the *Colloquies* was a book for boys, an answer that only made matters worse. He insisted that his dialogues were morally suitable as well as grammatically and rhetorically instructive for youth, scoffing at those who, he said, allowed boys to read the bawdy stories of Poggio but carped at the *Colloquies*.[30] It is fair to say that whatever coarseness or obscenity there may be in the *Colloquies* is confined to a few pages.

The second complaint was more serious, and more troublesome to answer. It charged that many scenes of religious life and many utterances on religion were impious or heretical.[31] Both Erasmus' words and the tone of those words were resented. His lively pages on the failings of monks and friars, his barbs at superstition and ignorance were bound to anger his persistent critics in the religious orders. Satire is sometimes a very effective social weapon, but the satirist must be prepared for counterattacks from those whose sensibilities he wounds or whose interests he endangers. As early as 1522, one of Erasmus' bitterest opponents, Nicholas Baechem (known as Egmondanus), Prior of the Carmelites at Louvain and also Inquisitor, wanted to burn the *Colloquies*, in which he believed he detected Lutheran heresies. More damaging than the opposition of a single official was that of the Sorbonne (the theological faculty of the University of Paris), the most celebrated and influential body of academic theologians in Europe. In May, 1526, the faculty censured the *Colloquies*,

---

[30] *Erasmi Epistolae*, VII, 492. 365-368.

[31] Luther denounced the author of the *Colloquies* as an atheistic mocker at religion, a modern Lucian who derided sacred things, and he is reported to have declared that on his deathbed he would forbid his sons to read Erasmus' *Colloquies* (*Tischreden*, Weimar edition, III, 136-137).

denouncing sixty-nine passages as questionable or heretical, and describing their author as a "pagan" who "mocked at the Christian religion and its sacred rites and customs." The book should be forbidden to all, especially to youth, said the faculty, lest under the pretext of instructing them it corrupt their morals.[32] When rumors of the Sorbonne's intentions reached him, Erasmus added to the June, 1526, edition of the *Colloquies* a letter to the reader, *De Utilitate Colloquiorum*. This defense of his book denies accusations of indecency; on the contrary, says Erasmus, he has improved his young readers by inculcating piety and good manners along with good Latin, and he has condemned only the abuses of religion.

At times his pages disturbed patrons or friends also. While they might approve of the purposes of his satire, they thought his language went too far, or that he was unfair and thus likely to do more harm than good. In April, 1526, shortly before the action of the Sorbonne, he took care to assure Cardinal Wolsey that the *Colloquies* contained nothing unclean, irreverent, or seditious.[33] A few years later Bishop Tunstall of London, a prelate who had long been favorably disposed toward Erasmus, objected to certain remarks on fasting, ceremonies, pilgrimages, and the invocation of saints.[34]

Censure of the book continued as long as Erasmus lived, and long afterwards. In 1538, the *Consilium . . . de Emendanda Ecclesia,* a scheme of reform drawn up by cardinals appointed by Pope Paul III, recommended that the *Colloquies* "and any other books of this sort" be prohibited.[35] When the Roman *Index Librorum Prohibitorum* was established, the *Colloquies* were in it, as they had been in earlier lists made by certain inquisitors, theological faculties, or synods. The Council of Trent condemned the entire *Colloquies* (1564). An *Index* of

[32] *Erasmi Opera Omnia* (Leiden edition), IX, 929C, A-B. The censure was not printed until 1531. In the following year Erasmus issued a reply in which he defended the passages one by one.

[33] *Erasmi Epistolae,* VI, 323. 62-63.

[34] *Ibid.,* VIII, 291. 56-62; cf. VI, 324. 73-80.

[35] *Documents Illustrative of the Continental Reformation,* ed. B. J. Kidd (1911), p. 315.

Paul IV (1559) had condemned all of Erasmus' commentaries, annotations, and translations as well as his *Colloquies*.[36]

A book enjoyed by so many, and yet offensive to others, must be valuable to any student of sixteenth-century thought and society. But it is not to be treated merely as a "source" for the information of historians. It is literature, and ought to be read and judged as literature. The present translation of ten representative colloquies is offered in the hope that readers interested in what Erasmus had to say may find useful a rendering into modern, informal English. It is made from the text of the Basel edition of the *Opera Omnia* (1540), although a Paris, 1533, text has been consulted occasionally. A translation of the entire *Colloquia,* with a commentary, is in preparation.

In the hands of Erasmus, Latin is no "dead" language but an instrument of thought and expression that is very much alive. The Latinity of the *Colloquies* is remarkably flexible in structure and tone, equally adaptable to dialogue, narrative, description; to sarcasm, banter, eloquence, or pathos. The difficulty of doing justice to this language in translation—that supreme risk for all literature—need not be pointed out to anyone who knows the original. So much felicity of style vanishes; so much of the wit goes lame. Yet a translator must hope to convey something of the spirit along with the sense of his author. If he fails, let him console himself with repeating what Erasmus says in the preface to his *Paraphrase of Hebrews:* "If you can't praise my wit and learning, at least give me credit for hard work." [37] Or the translator may echo the apology of one of his sixteenth-century predecessors, Nicholas Leigh: "Because I have changed his eloquent style into our English phrase, and thereby altered his livery, and embased the perfect grace of his Muse, I am compelled to crave pardon of this my doings. Consider, I beseech thee (learned reader), that if it had still rested in that noble

---

36 For details see the *Bibliotheca Erasmiana, passim;* F. H. Reusch, *Der Index der verbotenen Bücher* (1883-1885), I, 347-367.

37 *Erasmi Epistolae*, IV, 437. 24-26.

language wherein he left it, although thy knowledge had yielded thee greater felicity than this my travail can, yet thousands, which by this mine endeavor may draw out some sweet sap of these his pleasant and fruitful doings, might (through ignorance) have wanted this piece of delight. Therefore the offense (if any be) is made to Erasmus, a man of that patience in his life as I assure myself that this my bold dealing with him cannot a whit disquiet his ghost." [38]

For assistance of various kinds I wish to thank Dr. Louis B. Wright, Isabella M. Thompson, and Professors Moses Hadas, Charles Brooks, and M. P. Cunningham. I am much indebted to Professor John F. Latimer for reading a draft of the translation and suggesting certain improvements.

CRAIG R. THOMPSON

[38] Leigh translated two colloquies, *Proci et Puellae* (translated in the present volume as "The Wooer and the Maiden") and *Adolescentis et Scorti*. These were published together, as *A Modest Meane to Mariage*, in 1568.

SELECTED BIBLIOGRAPHY

COLLECTED WORKS OF ERASMUS

Erasmi Opera Omnia. Basel, 1540.

Erasmi Opera Omnia. Edited by J. Clericus. Leiden, 1703-06. (Cited in the notes as "Leiden edition.")

Desiderius Erasmus Roterodamus, Ausgewählte Werke. Edited by H. Holborn. Munich, 1933.

Erasmi Opuscula. Edited by W. K. Ferguson. The Hague, 1933.

Opus Epistolarum Des. Erasmi Roterodami. Edited by P. S. Allen, H. M. Allen, H. W. Garrod. Oxford, 1906-47. (Cited in the notes as *Erasmi Epistolae.*)

Bibliotheca Erasmiana, Vols. IV-VI: *Colloquia.* Edited by F. van der Haeghen. Ghent, 1903-07.

LIFE AND TIMES OF ERASMUS

Allen, P. S. *The Age of Erasmus.* Oxford, 1914.

—————. *Erasmus: Lectures and Wayfaring Sketches.* Oxford, 1934.

Chambers, R. W. *Thomas More.* London, 1935.

Froude, R. W. *Life and Letters of Erasmus.* New York, 1894.

Gedenkschrift zum 400. Todestage des Erasmus von Rotterdam. Basel, 1936.

Huizinga, J. *Erasmus of Rotterdam.* Translated by F. Hopman. New York, 1924.

Hyma, A. *The Youth of Erasmus.* Ann Arbor, Mich., 1930.

Phillips, M. M. *Erasmus and the Northern Renaissance.* London, 1949.

Renaudet, A. *Erasme, sa pensée religieuse.* Paris, 1926.

—————. *Etudes érasmiennes.* Paris, 1939.

Smith, P. *Erasmus.* New York, 1923.

—————. *A Key to the Colloquies of Erasmus.* Cambridge, Mass., 1927.

TEN COLLOQUIES

THE SHIPWRECK

First printed 1523. Although "The Shipwreck" is mainly the achievement of Erasmus' artistic imagination, some passages contain recollections of the disaster described in Acts 27. It is possible, moreover, that Erasmus had in mind a shipwreck that occurred off the coast of Friesland in 1516. For the evidence see Preserved Smith, *A Key to the Colloquies of Erasmus* (1927), pp. 19-20.

This was one of the most popular of all the *Colloquies*. Rabelais (*Gargantua and Pantagruel,* Bk. IV, chs. 18-22), and Reade (*The Cloister and the Hearth,* ch. 57) borrowed from it. Thomas Heywood translated it into rhymed verse (*Dialogues,* 1637).

ANTONY, ADOLPH

Antony. Terrible tales you tell! That's what going to sea is like? God forbid any such notion should ever enter *my* head!

Adolph. Oh, no, what I've related up to this point is mere sport compared with what you'll hear now.

Antony. I've heard more than enough of disasters. When you're recalling them I shudder as if I myself were sharing the danger.

Adolph. To me, on the contrary, troubles over and done with are enjoyable.—On that same night something happened which in large part robbed the skipper of his hope of safety.

Antony. What, I beseech you?

Adolph. The night was partially clear, and on the topmast, in the "crow's-nest" (as I think they call it), stood one of the crew, looking out for land. Suddenly a fiery ball [1] appeared beside him—a very bad sign to sailors when it's a single

[1] The electrical phenomenon called St. Elmo's fire.

3

flame, lucky when it's double. Antiquity believed these were Castor and Pollux.

Antony. What's their connection with sailors? One was a horseman, the other a boxer.

Adolph. This is the poets' version. The skipper, who was by the helm, spoke up: "Mate"—that's what sailors call one another—"see your company alongside there?" "I see it," the man replied, "and I hope it's good luck." Soon the blazing ball slid down the ropes and rolled straight up to the skipper.

Antony. Wasn't he scared out of his wits?

Adolph. Sailors get used to marvels. After stopping there a moment, it rolled the whole way round the ship, then dropped through the middle hatches and disappeared. Toward noon the storm began to rage more and more. Ever seen the Alps?

Antony. Yes, I've seen them.

Adolph. Those mountains are warts compared with the waves of the sea. Whenever we were borne on the crest, we could have touched the moon with a finger; whenever dipped, we seemed to plunge through the gaping earth to hell.

Antony. What fools they are who trust themselves to the sea!

Adolph. Since the crew's struggle with the storm was hopeless, the skipper, pale as a ghost, at last came up to us.

Antony. His pallor forebodes some great disaster.

Adolph. "Friends," he says, "I'm no longer master of my ship; the winds have won. The only thing left to do is to put our hope in God and each one prepare himself for the end."

Antony. Truly a Scythian [2] speech.

Adolph. "But first of all," he says, "the ship must be unloaded. Necessity, a stern foe, demands it. Better to save life at the cost of goods than for both to perish together." This was undeniable. A lot of luggage filled with costly wares was tossed overboard.

Antony. This was sacrificing for sure!

2 Blunt, harsh.

Adolph. On board was a certain Italian who had served as legate to the King of Scotland. He had a chest full of silver plate, rings, cloth, and silk robes.

Antony. He didn't want to come to terms with the sea?

Adolph. No, instead he wanted to go down with his beloved treasures or else be saved along with them. So he protested.

Antony. What did the skipper do?

Adolph. "We're quite willing to let you perish alone with your goods," said he, "but it's not fair for all of us to be endangered because of your chest. What's more, we'll throw you and the chest together into the sea."

Antony. True sailor's lingo!

Adolph. So the Italian, too, threw his goods overboard, cursing away by heaven and hell because he had entrusted his life to so barbarous an element.[3]

Antony. I recognize the Italian accent.

Adolph. Soon afterward the winds, unappeased by our offerings, broke the ropes and tore the sails to pieces.

Antony. Catastrophe!

Adolph. At that moment the skipper comes to us again.

Antony. To make a speech?

Adolph. "Friends"—he begins by way of greeting—"the hour warns each of us to commend himself to God and prepare for death." Questioned by some who were familiar with seamanship as to how many hours he thought he could keep the ship afloat, he replied that he couldn't promise anything, but not more than three hours.

Antony. This speech was even sterner than the first one.

Adolph. After saying this, he orders all the shrouds to be slashed and the mast sawn off down to its socket and thrown into the sea, together with the spars.

Antony. Why this?

Adolph. With the sail ruined or torn, the mast was a useless burden. Our whole hope was in the tiller.

[3] As Erasmus remarks in his *Praise of Folly,* everything foreign was "barbarous" to Italians.

Antony. What about the passengers meanwhile?

Adolph. There you'd have seen what a wretched plight we were in: the sailors singing *Salve Regina,* praying to the Virgin Mother, calling her Star of the Sea, Queen of Heaven, Mistress of the World, Port of Salvation, flattering her with many other titles the Sacred Scriptures nowhere assign to her.[4]

Antony. What has she to do with the sea? She never went voyaging, I believe.

Adolph. Formerly Venus was protectress of sailors, because she was believed to have been born of the sea. Since she gave up guarding them, the Virgin Mother has succeeded this mother who was not a virgin.

Antony. You're joking.

Adolph. Prostrating themselves on the deck, some worshiped the sea, pouring whatever oil they had on the waves, flattering it no differently from the way we do a wrathful sovereign.

Antony. What did they say?

Adolph. "O most merciful sea, O most kind sea, O most splendid sea, O most lovely sea, have pity on us! Save us!" Many songs of this kind they sang to the sea—which was deaf.

Antony. Absurd superstition! What did the rest do?

Adolph. Some did nothing but get sick. Many made vows. There was an Englishman who promised heaps of gold to the Virgin of Walsingham [5] if he reached shore alive. Some promised many things to the wood of the Cross at such and such a place; others, again, to that in some other place. The same with respect to the Virgin Mary, who reigns in many places; and they think the vow worthless unless you specify the place.

Antony. Ridiculous! As if saints don't dwell in heaven.

---

4 Erasmus' ecclesiastical and academic enemies denounced this and other passages in "The Shipwreck" as impious. Erasmus retorted that he was attacking superstitions (*Opera Omnia,* Leiden edition, IX, 942C-943F, 1086C-F, 1163C-E).

5 On the gold at the shrine of Walsingham, and the wood of the Cross, see "A Pilgrimage for Religion's Sake."

Adolph. Some pledged themselves to become Carthusians. There was one who promised to journey to St. James at Compostella [6] barefoot, bareheaded, clad only in a coat of mail, begging his bread besides.

Antony. Did nobody remember Christopher? [7]

Adolph. I couldn't help laughing as I listened to one chap, who in a loud voice (for fear he wouldn't be heard) promised a wax taper as big as himself to the Christopher in the tallest church in Paris—a mountain rather than a statue. While he was proclaiming this at the top of his lungs, insisting on it again and again, an acquaintance who chanced to be standing by nudged him with his elbow and cautioned: "Be careful what you promise. Even if you sold all your goods at auction, you couldn't pay for it." Then the other, lowering his voice—so St. Christopher wouldn't overhear him, of course! —said, "Shut up, you fool. Do you suppose I'm serious? If I once touch land, I won't give him a tallow candle."

Antony. O stupid! I suspect he was a Batavian.[8]

Adolph. No, but he was a Zeelander.

Antony. I'm surprised nobody thought of the Apostle Paul, who was once shipwrecked himself, and when the ship broke, jumped overboard and reached land.[9] No stranger to misfortune, he knew how to help those in distress.

Adolph. Paul wasn't mentioned.

Antony. Did they pray all the while?

Adolph. Strenuously. One chanted *Salve Regina,* another *Credo in Deum.* Some had certain queer beads,[10] like charms, to ward off danger.

Antony. How devout men are made by suffering! In prosperity the thought of God or saint never enters their heads.

[6] In northwestern Spain. One of the favorite places of pilgrimage in the Middle Ages.

[7] Patron saint of travelers. The statue mentioned a few lines later once stood in the entrance of the Church of Notre Dame.

[8] Erasmus enjoyed a joke at the expense of his fellow Hollanders, but note his remark, at the end of the colloquy, about their character.

[9] Acts 27:9-44.

[10] Rosaries.

What were you doing all this time? Making vows to any of the saints?

Adolph. Not at all.

Antony. Why?

Adolph. Because I don't make deals with saints. For what else is that but a bargain according to the form "I'll give this if you do that" or "I'll do this if you'll do that"; "I'll give a taper if I can swim"; "I'll go to Rome if you save me."

Antony. But you called on some saint for help?

Adolph. Not even that.

Antony. But why?

Adolph. Because heaven's a large place. If I entrust my safety to some saint—St. Peter, for example, who perhaps will be the first to hear, since he stands at the gate—I may be dead before he meets God and pleads my cause.

Antony. What did you do, then?

Adolph. Went straight to the Father himself, reciting the Pater Noster. No saint hears sooner than he, or more willingly grants what is asked.

Antony. But didn't your conscience accuse you when you did this? Weren't you afraid to entreat the Father, whom you had offended by so many sins?

Adolph. To speak frankly, my conscience did deter me somewhat. But I soon recovered my spirits, thinking to myself, "No father is so angry with his son that, if he sees him in danger in a stream or lake, he won't grasp him by the hair and pull him out." Of all the passengers, none behaved more calmly than a certain woman who was suckling a baby.

Antony. What did she do?

Adolph. She was the only one who didn't scream, weep, or make promises; she simply prayed in silence, clasping her little boy. While the ship was continually battered by the sea, the skipper undergirded it with ropes both fore and aft, for fear it might break to pieces.

Antony. Miserable protection!

Adolph. Meantime an old priest, a man of sixty named Adam, jumped up. Stripped to his underclothes, and with his shoes and leggings removed, he urged us all to prepare likewise for swimming. And standing so in the middle of the ship, he preached to us a sermon from Gerson [11] on the five truths concerning the benefit of confession. He urged everyone to be ready both for life and for death. A Dominican was there, too. Those who wished confessed to these two.

Antony. What did you do?

Adolph. Seeing everything in an uproar, I confessed silently to God, condemning my unrighteousness before him and imploring his mercy.

Antony. Where would you have gone if you had died in that condition?

Adolph. That I left to God the judge, for I was unwilling to be judge of my own cause; nevertheless a strong hope possessed my mind the whole time. While all this is going on, the captain tearfully returns to us. "Get ready," says he, "because the ship will be useless to us in a quarter of an hour." For it was already shattered in some places, and was drawing water. Soon afterwards a sailor reports seeing a church tower in the distance, and beseeches us to appeal to whichever saint took that church under his protection. Everyone falls to his knees and prays to the unknown saint.

Antony. Had you invoked him by name, he might have heard.

Adolph. We didn't know his name. As much as he could, meantime, the skipper steered the ship in that direction. It was already breaking up, taking in water everywhere and clearly about to fall to pieces if it hadn't been undergirded with ropes.

Antony. A bad state of affairs!

Adolph. We were carried far enough in for the inhabitants of the place to see our plight. Groups of them rushed to the shore, and taking off hats and coats and sticking them on poles, urged us towards themselves, and by lifting their arms to heaven indicated their pity for our lot.

[11] The great churchman and chancellor of the University of Paris (1363-1429); famous as a theologian and preacher.

Antony. I'm waiting to hear what happened.

Adolph. The whole ship was filled with water now, so that thereafter we would be no safer in ship than in sea.

Antony. At that moment you had to fall back on your last hope.

Adolph. On suffering, rather. The crew released the lifeboat and lowered it into the sea. Everyone tried to hurl himself into it, the sailors protesting in the uproar that the lifeboat would not hold such a crowd, but everybody should grab what he could and swim. The situation did not allow leisurely plans. One person snatched an oar, another a boathook, another a tub, another a bucket, another a plank; and, each relying on his own resources, they committed themselves to the waves.

Antony. What happened during this time to that poor little woman who alone did not weep and wail?

Adolph. She was the first of them all to reach shore.

Antony. How could she do that?

Adolph. We put her on a curved plank and tied her in such a way that she couldn't easily fall off. We gave her a small board to use as a paddle, and, wishing her luck, shoved her off into the waves, pushing with a pole to get her clear of the ship, where the danger lay. Holding her baby in her left hand, she paddled with the right.

Antony. Brave woman!

Adolph. Since nothing else remained, one man seized a wooden statue of the Virgin Mother, now rotten and mouse-eaten, and, putting his arms around it, began to swim.

Antony. Did the lifeboat come through safely?

Adolph. The first to go down. And thirty people had thrown themselves into it.

Antony. What mishap caused that?

Adolph. Before it could get away it was overturned by the lurching of the big ship.

Antony. A cruel business! What then?

Adolph. While looking out for others, I nearly perished myself.

Antony. How so?

Adolph. Because there was nothing left for me to swim on.

Antony. Cork would have been useful there.

Adolph. In that emergency I would rather have had plain cork tree than golden candlestick. Casting about, I finally thought of the stump of the mast. Since I couldn't pry it loose by myself, I enlisted the help of another man. Supporting ourselves on this, we put to sea, I holding on to the right end and he to the left. While we were tossing about in this way, that priest who preached on board threw himself in our midst —on our shoulders. Big fellow, too. "Who's the third?" we yell. "He'll be the death of us all." He, on the other hand, says calmly, "Cheer up, there's plenty of room. God will help us."

Antony. Why was he so late in starting to swim?

Adolph. Oh, he was to be in the lifeboat along with the Dominican (for everybody conceded this much honor to him), but although they had confessed to each other on the ship, nevertheless some condition—I don't know what—had been forgotten. There on the edge of the ship they confess anew, and each lays his hand on the other. While they're doing this, the lifeboat goes down. Adam told me this.

Antony. What became of the Dominican?

Adolph. According to Adam, after entreating the aid of the saints he threw off his clothes and began to swim.

Antony. Which saints did he invoke?

Adolph. Dominic, Thomas, Vincent, and I don't know which Peter, but first and foremost he placed his trust in Catherine of Siena.

Antony. Christ didn't come to mind?

Adolph. This is what the priest told me.

Antony. He'd have swum better if he hadn't thrown off his sacred cowl. With that put aside, how could Catherine of Siena recognize him? But go on with what happened to you.

Adolph. While we were still tossing beside the ship, which was rolling from side to side at the will of the waves, the broken rudder smashed the thigh of the man who was holding on to the left end of the stump. So he was torn away. The priest, saying a prayer *Requiem aeternam* for him, took his place, urging me to keep hold of my end with confidence and kick my feet vigorously. We were swallowing a lot of salt water all this while. Thus Neptune saw to it that we had not only a salty bath but even a salty drink, though the priest showed us a remedy for that.

Antony. What, please?

Adolph. Every time a wave came rushing upon us, he turned the back of his head to it and kept his mouth closed.

Antony. A doughty old fellow you tell me of.

Adolph. When we'd made some progress after swimming a while, the priest, who was very tall, said, "Cheer up, I'm touching bottom!" I didn't dare hope for such great luck. "We're too far from shore to hope for bottom." "Oh, no," he replied, "I feel land with my feet." "Maybe it's something from the chests that the sea has rolled this way." "No," he said, "I feel land plainly by the scraping of my toes." After we had swum a while longer in this direction and he again touched bottom, "Do what you think best," he said, "I'm giving up the whole mast to you and trusting myself to the bottom"; and thereupon, after waiting for the waves to subside, he went on foot as fast as he could. When the waves overtook him again, he resisted by clasping his knees with his hands and putting his head under water, as divers and ducks do; when the waves receded, up he popped and rushed on. When I saw he was successful at this, I imitated him. Standing on the coast were men—hardy fellows, and used to the water—who by means of extremely long poles, held out from one to the other, braced themselves against the force of the waves; so that the one farthest out held his pole to the swimmer. When this was grasped, all heaved toward shore and the swimmer was hauled safely to dry land. A number were rescued by this device.

Antony. How many?

Adolph. Seven, but two of these died when brought to a fire.

Antony. How many were you in the ship?

Adolph. Fifty-eight.

Antony. O cruel sea! At least it might have been satisfied with a tenth, which is enough for priests. From so large a number how few returned!

Adolph. We were treated with wonderful kindness by the people there, who looked after our needs with astonishing eagerness: lodging, fire, food, clothing, money for travel.

Antony. What people were they?

Adolph. Hollanders.

Antony. No people could be more kindly, though they do have savage neighbors. I guess you won't visit Neptune very soon again after this.

Adolph. No, not unless God takes my reason from me.

Antony. And I for my part would rather hear such tales than experience the events at first hand.

❧ II ☙
INNS

First printed 1523. Erasmus complains occasionally in his letters, as he does in this colloquy, about the discomfort of German inns and the rudeness of German people. His memories of the more pleasant inn in Lyons went back to 1506, when he stopped there on his way to Italy.

Hilary Bertulf was one of his servant-pupils. He appears as interlocutor in several other colloquies.

Scott used this colloquy in *Anne of Geierstein,* chapter 19; Reade in *The Cloister and the Hearth,* chapters 24 and 33.

BERTULF, WILLIAM

Bertulf. Why do most people like to linger two or three days in Lyons? Once *I've* started on a journey I don't rest until I've reached my destination.

William. On the contrary, I marvel that anybody can tear himself away from there.

Bertulf. Just why is that?

William. Because of a place there that the companions of Ulysses couldn't have been torn away from. The Sirens are there. No one's treated better in his own home than in a public house in Lyons.

Bertulf. What happens?

William. At the table some woman would always be standing by to enliven the meal with jokes and pleasantries (and the women there are awfully good-looking, too). First the hostess would come and welcome us, bidding us be merry and accept with good grace whatever was served. After her the daughter, a lovely woman with such delightful manners and speech that she would cheer Cato [1] himself. They would chat with us not as with strangers, but as if with old familiar friends.

Bertulf. I know the politeness of the French.

William. But since they couldn't be present continuously —because there were chores to be looked after, and other guests greeted—we were attended the whole time by a young miss who was well prepared for all the jokes, quite able to handle unassisted all the jests directed her way. She kept the talk going until the daughter returned; for the mother was rather old.

Bertulf. But precisely what was the food like? Because stories don't fill your belly.

William. Really sumptuous; so sumptuous I wonder they can take guests for so low a price. Again, when the meal is finished they feast a man with funny stories, so he won't become bored. I fancied myself at home, not abroad.

Bertulf. What did you find in the bedrooms?

William. Girls: laughing, jolly, sportive girls everywhere. They asked of their own accord if we had any dirty clothes; they washed them and brought them back—clean. In short, we saw nothing there but women and girls except in the stable, though often girls invaded even that. They embrace the departing guests and take leave of them as affectionately as if they were all brothers or close relatives.

Bertulf. Maybe these manners suit the French. I prefer German ones, as being more manly.

William. I've never seen Germany, as it happens, so please do be good enough to tell me how a guest is treated there.

Bertulf. Whether the method of treatment is the same everywhere, I don't know. I'll tell you what I saw. No one greets the arrival, lest they seem to be looking for a guest. For that they consider base and degrading, and unworthy of Germanic austerity. When you've shouted a long time, some-

---

[1] Marcus Porcius Cato, called "Cato the Censor" or the "Elder" (234-149 B.C.), who tried to bring back by legislation a very stern moral standard.

one finally sticks his head out of the little window of the stove room ² (where they spend most of their time until midsummer), like a turtle from his shell. You must ask him if you may put up there. If he doesn't shake his head, you know there's room for you. Those who ask where the stable is are directed by a wave of the hand. There you may look after your horse as you like, for no servant lifts a finger. Though if the inn's one of the better-known ones, a servant does show you the stable and even a place for your horse—a very poor place, since the better ones are reserved for the use of later guests, especially nobility. If you ask why, you hear instantly, "If you don't like this, look for another inn." In the cities they furnish hay very reluctantly and sparingly, and it costs almost as much as oats itself. When the horse is provided for, you move into the stove room with all your impedimenta—leggings, luggage, and mud (which is one thing all travelers have in common).

William. At French inns guests are shown to a chamber where they may undress, dry and warm themselves, or even rest if they wish.

Bertulf. Nothing of the sort here. In the stove room you take off leggings, put on shoes, change underwear if you like; rain-drenched clothing you hang beside the stove, and you move there yourself in order to dry out. If you want to wash your hands, water is brought, but usually it's so clean that afterward you have to look for other water to wash it off with!

William. I approve of men who aren't made effeminate by luxuries.

Bertulf. But if you arrive at four o'clock, still you won't dine before nine and sometimes ten.

William. Why?

Bertulf. They don't prepare anything unless they see everyone's present, in order to serve them all in one operation.

---

² The heated—and, in Erasmus' opinion, usually overheated—public room of the inn. Erasmus detested such rooms and often complained about them. *Alemanica hypocausta* deterred him, he said, from living in Germany.

William. Looking for a short cut.

Bertulf. Exactly. Thus there are often eighty or ninety met together in the same stove room: travelers afoot, horsemen, traders, sailors, carriers, farmers, young men, women, the sick and the whole.

William. The common life with a vengeance!

Bertulf. One combs his hair, another wipes the sweat off, another cleans his rawhide boots or his leggings, another belches garlic. To make a long story short, the confusion of tongues and people there is equal to that long ago in the tower of Babel. But if they set eyes on a foreigner, whose dress gives him an air of distinction, they all stare intently at him, gazing as if at some new species of animal imported from Africa. This is carried so far that after they've sat down at table they turn round and continue to stare, not taking their eyes off him; they forget to eat.

William. At Rome, Paris, and Venice nothing surprises anybody.

Bertulf. You're not allowed to ask for anything meanwhile. When the evening's already late and no more arrivals are expected, an aged servant with white beard, cropped head, grim look, and dirty clothes makes his appearance.

William. Just the sort to be cupbearer to Roman cardinals.

Bertulf. Glancing round, he silently counts the people in the stove room. The more he sees there, the more energetically he fires up the stove, even though the weather is oppressively warm without it. Among these folk it's a principal part of good management to melt everybody in sweat. If someone not used to steam should open a window to escape suffocation, he hears instantly, "Close it!" If you reply, "I can't stand this," they tell you, "Then look for another inn."

William. But nothing seems to me more dangerous than for so many persons to breathe the same warm air, especially when their bodies are relaxed and they've eaten together and stayed in the same place a good many hours. Not to mention the belching of garlic, the breaking of wind, the stinking breaths, many persons suffer from hidden diseases, and every disease is contagious. Undoubtedly many have the Spanish or, as some call it, French pox,[3] though it's common to all countries. In my opinion, there's almost as much danger from these men as from lepers. Just imagine, now, how great the risk of plague.

Bertulf. They're brave fellows. They laugh at these things and pay no attention to them.

William. But all the while their bravery endangers the public.

Bertulf. What would you do? This is their custom, and they're resolved not to depart from established ways.

William. Twenty-five years ago nothing was more customary among the Brabanters than public steam baths. Now these are out of fashion everywhere, for the new pox has taught us to let them alone.

Bertulf. But hear the rest. After a while the bearded Ganymede [4] returns and lays the linen for as many tables as he thinks sufficient for the number of diners. But good God! far from Milesian linen—you'd say hemp pulled off sailyards. Guests are directed to every single table, eight at least to each one. Now those familiar with native custom sit down wherever they please, for there's no distinction between rich and poor, master and servant.

William. That old-time equality, abolished by modern tyranny! In my opinion, Christ lived thus with his disciples.

Bertulf. After they're all seated, our gloomy Ganymede appears again and counts his company once more. Coming back shortly, he places beside each one a wooden dish, and a spoon made of the same silver, then a glass cup; later on, bread, which everyone cleans up leisurely while the porridge is cooking. Sometimes you sit and wait almost an hour.

William. None of the guests demands food during this time?

Bertulf. None who's acquainted with the temper of the

3 Syphilis.

4 In Greek mythology, a handsome boy, carried off to heaven to be cupbearer to Zeus.

country. At last the wine is served—good Lord, anything but
mellow! Sophisters would need no other drink, so sharp and
pungent is it. But if some guest, even offering a tip on the
side, asks them to find him another kind of wine, at first they
ignore him, but looking as if they're about to murder him. If
you press them, they'll reply, "So many counts and marquises
have stayed here, and not one of them complained about my
wine. If you don't like it, look for another inn." For they regard only their own native nobility as men, and display their
coats of arms everywhere. — So now the guests have a morsel
to toss to the barking stomach. Soon afterwards, amidst much
ceremony, dishes arrive. The first generally has bits of bread
dipped in meat broth; or, if it's fish day, in bean juice. Next
another broth; after that some warmed-over meat or salt fish.
Again porridge, followed by more solid food; next they serve
the thoroughly tamed stomach roast meat or boiled fish that
you could not altogether scorn—but they're stingy with this,
and quickly remove it. They arrange the whole meal in this
fashion, alternating solid food and pulse, as actors alternate
choruses and dramatic scenes. But they take care to make the
last act the best.

William. The sign of a good poet, too.

Bertulf. Moreover, it's sacrilege to say, "Take this dish
away; nobody's eating it." You must sit there the appointed
length of time, which I fancy they measure by water clocks.
Finally our bearded chap turns up; or the innkeeper himself,
whose dress differs very little from that of the servants. He
asks what we would like. Soon some rather better wine is
brought. They admire heavy drinkers, although the one who
downs the most wine pays no more than the one who drinks
the least.

William. A strange characteristic of the race.

Bertulf. At times, however, some spend on wine more
than twice the cost of their dinner. But (before I finish with
this feast) the uproar and tumult after they've all begun to
grow heated from drink is astonishing. In short, it's completely
deafening. Often jesters mingle with the guests. Despite the

fact that no class of men is more detestable, you'd scarcely believe how fond of them the Germans are: they sing, chatter, shout, dance, and stamp, until the stove room seems about to collapse. You can't hear a word anybody else is saying. Yet all the while they think they're having the time of their lives, and you must sit there until midnight whether you want to or not.

William. Finish the feast at last now. For such a long-drawn-out affair bores me, too.

Bertulf. I will. When the cheese—which is hardly acceptable to them unless full of mold and worms—is finally taken away, the bearded chap comes in carrying a tray on which he's chalked some circles and half-circles. This he places on the table in grim silence—you'd say he was a Charon.[5] Those familiar with the scene lay down money, one man after another, until the tray is filled. Then, after checking those who've paid, he counts the money to himself. If nothing's lacking, he nods his head.

William. What if something's left over?

Bertulf. Maybe he'd return it. They do, sometimes.

William. Does no one protest against this villainous system?

Bertulf. No one in his right mind. For instantly he'd hear, "What sort of man are you? You don't pay any more than the rest here."

William. These are blunt folk you tell of.

Bertulf. But if someone tired out from travel wants to go to bed soon after dinner, he's told to wait until others go, too.

William. Plato's republic, it seems.

Bertulf. Then everyone is shown his nest; actually a mere cubicle, for it contains only beds and nothing else you could use or steal.

William. Is it clean?

Bertulf. Like the dinner; the linen washed perhaps six months before.

William. What about the horses, meantime?

[5] Charon's office is to ferry the souls of the dead over the Styx.

Bertulf. They're treated on the same principle as the men.

William. But is this treatment the same everywhere?

Bertulf. In some places it's more civil, in others rougher than that I've described. But in general it's like this.

William. What if I were to tell you now how guests are treated in that region of Italy called Lombardy, again in Spain, then in England and Wales? For the English follow in part the French custom, in part the German, as they're a mixture of these two peoples. The Welsh boast themselves the native English.

Bertulf. I beg you to tell me, because I've never had opportunity to visit them.

William. Haven't time just now, for the sailor bade me be on hand at three o'clock if I didn't want to be left behind, and he has my luggage. There'll be opportunity some other time to have our fill of talk.

THE WOOER AND THE MAIDEN

First printed 1523. For other treatments of love and marriage see *Encomium Matrimonii* (1518), *Christiani Matrimonii Institutio* (1526)—dedicated to Catherine of Aragon, Queen of England—and the colloquy *Coniugium* (1523). The place of these writings in Renaissance and Reformation discussions of marriage is examined in E. V. Telle's *Erasme de Rotterdam et le septième sacrement* (1954).

This colloquy was criticized for its freedom of language. For Erasmus' defense see *Erasmi Epistolae*, VII, 460. 22-26, his *De Utilitate Colloquiorum* (1526), and *Opera Omnia*, Leiden edition, IX, 937C—938A.

PAMPHILUS, MARIA

Pamphilus. Hello—you cruel, hardhearted, unrelenting creature!

Maria. Hello yourself, Pamphilus, as often and as much as you like, and by whatever name you please. But sometimes I think you've forgotten my name. It's Maria.

Pamphilus. Quite appropriate for *you* to be named after Mars.

Maria. Why so? What have I to do with Mars?

Pamphilus. You slay men for sport, as the god does. Except that you're more pitiless than Mars: you kill even a lover.

Maria. Mind what you're saying. Where's this heap of men I've slain? Where's the blood of the slaughtered?

Pamphilus. You've only to look at me to see one lifeless corpse.

Maria. What do I hear? You speak and walk about when you're dead? I hope I never meet more fearsome ghosts!

Pamphilus. You're joking, but all the same you're the

death of poor me, and you kill more cruelly than if you pierced with a spear. Now, alas, I'm just skin and bones from long torture.

Maria. Well, well! Tell me, how many pregnant women have miscarried at the sight of you?

Pamphilus. But my pallor shows I've less blood than any ghost.

Maria. Yet this pallor is streaked with lavender. You're as pale as a ripening cherry or a purple grape.

Pamphilus. Shame on you for making fun of a miserable wretch!

Maria. But if you don't believe me, bring a mirror.

Pamphilus. I want no other mirror, nor do I think any could be brighter, than the one in which I'm looking at myself now.

Maria. What mirror are you talking about?

Pamphilus. Your eyes.

Maria. Quibbler! Just like you! But how do you prove you're lifeless? Do ghosts eat?

Pamphilus. Yes, but they eat insipid stuff, as I do.

Maria. What do they eat, then?

Pamphilus. Mallows, leeks, and lupines.

Maria. But you don't abstain from capons and partridges.

Pamphilus. True, but they taste no better to my palate than if I were eating mallows, or beets without pepper, wine, and vinegar.

Maria. Poor you! Yet all the time you're growing rather stout. And do dead men talk?

Pamphilus. Like me, in a very thin, squeaky voice.

Maria. When I heard you wrangling with your rival not long ago, though, your voice wasn't so thin and squeaky. But, I ask you, do ghosts even walk? Wear clothes? Sleep?

Pamphilus. They even copulate, but after their own fashion.

Maria. Well! Clever rogue, aren't you?

Pamphilus. But what will you say if I demonstrate with Achillean proofs that I'm dead and you're a murderer?

Maria. Perish the thought, Pamphilus! But proceed to your argument.

Pamphilus. In the first place, you'll grant, I suppose, that death is nothing but removal of soul from body?

Maria. Granted.

Pamphilus. But grant it so that you won't want to take back what you've given.

Maria. I won't want to.

Pamphilus. Then, you won't deny that whoever deprives another of his soul is a murderer?

Maria. I allow it.

Pamphilus. You'll concede also what's affirmed by the most respected authors, and endorsed by the assent of so many ages: that man's soul is not where it animates but where it loves.

Maria. Explain this more simply. I don't quite follow your meaning.

Pamphilus. And the worse for me that you don't see this as clearly as I do.

Maria. Try to make me see it.

Pamphilus. As well try to make adamant see!

Maria. Well, I'm a girl, not a stone.

Pamphilus. True, but harder than adamant.

Maria. But get on with your argument.

Pamphilus. Men seized by a divine inspiration neither hear nor see nor smell nor feel, even if you kill them.

Maria. Yes, I've heard that.

Pamphilus. What do you suppose is the reason?

Maria. You tell me, professor.

Pamphilus. Obviously because their spirit is in heaven, where it possesses what it ardently loves, and is absent from the body.

Maria. What of it?

Pamphilus. What of it, you unfeeling girl? It follows both that I'm dead and that you're the murderer.

Maria. Where's your soul, then?

Pamphilus. Where it loves.

Maria. But who robbed you of your soul? What are you sighing for? Speak freely; I won't hold it against you.

Pamphilus. Cruelest of girls, whom nevertheless I can't hate even if I'm dead!

Maria. Naturally. But why don't you in turn deprive her of *her* soul—tit for tat, as they say?

Pamphilus. I'd like nothing better if the exchange could be such that her spirit migrated to my breast, as my spirit has gone over completely to her body.

Maria. But may I, in my turn, play the sophist with you?

Pamphilus. The sophistress.

Maria. It isn't possible for the same body to be living and lifeless, is it?

Pamphilus. No, not at the same time.

Maria. When the soul's gone, then the body's dead?

Pamphilus. Yes.

Maria. It doesn't animate except when it's present?

Pamphilus. Exactly.

Maria. Then how does it happen that although the soul's there where it loves, it nevertheless animates the body left behind? If it animates that body even when it loves elsewhere, how can the animated body be called lifeless?

Pamphilus. You dispute cunningly enough, but you won't catch me with such snares. The soul that somehow or other governs the body of a lover [1] is incorrectly called soul, since actually it consists of certain slight remnants of soul—just as the scent of roses remains in your hand even if the rose is taken away.

Maria. Hard to catch a fox with a noose, I see! But answer me this: doesn't one who kills perform an act?

Pamphilus. Of course.

Maria. And the one who's killed suffers?

Pamphilus. Yes indeed.

Maria. Then how is it that although the lover is active and the beloved passive, the beloved is said to kill—when the lover, rather, kills himself?

[1] Reading *amantis* for *animantis.*

Pamphilus. On the contrary, it's the lover who suffers; the beloved does the deed.

Maria. You'll never win this case before the supreme court of grammarians.

Pamphilus. But I'll win it before the congress of logicians.

Maria. Now don't begrudge an answer to this, too: do you love willingly or unwillingly?

Pamphilus. Willingly.

Maria. Then since one is free not to love, whoever loves seems to be a self-murderer. To blame the girl is unjust.

Pamphilus. Yet the girl doesn't kill by being loved, but by failing to return the love. Whoever can save someone and refrains from doing so is guilty of murder.

Maria. Suppose a young man loves what is forbidden, for example another man's wife or a Vestal Virgin? She won't return his love in order to save the lover, will she?

Pamphilus. But *this* young man loves what it's lawful and right, and reasonable and honorable, to love; and yet he's slain. If this crime of murder is trivial, I'll bring a charge of poisoning too.

Maria. Heaven forbid! Will you make a Circe of me?

Pamphilus. Something more pitiless than that. For I'd rather be a hog or a bear than what I am now, a lifeless thing.

Maria. Well, just what sort of poison do I kill men with?

Pamphilus. You charm them.

Maria. Then you want me to keep my poisonous eyes off you hereafter?

Pamphilus. Don't say such things! No, turn them on me more and more.

Maria. If my eyes are charmers, why don't the other men I look at languish, too? So I suspect this witchcraft is in your own eyes, not in mine.

Pamphilus. Wasn't it enough to slay Pamphilus without mocking him besides?

Maria. A handsome corpse! But when's the funeral?

Pamphilus. Sooner than you think—unless you rescue me.

Maria. Have I so much power?

Pamphilus. You can bring a dead man back to life, and that with little trouble.

Maria. If someone gave me a cure-all.

Pamphilus. No need of medicines; just return his love. What could be easier or fairer? In no other way will you be acquitted of the crime of homicide.

Maria. Before which court shall I be tried? That of the Areopagites? [2]

Pamphilus. No, the court of Venus.

Maria. She's an easygoing goddess, they say.

Pamphilus. Oh no, her wrath's the most terrible of all.

Maria. Has she a thunderbolt?

Pamphilus. No.

Maria. A trident?

Pamphilus. By no means.

Maria. Has she a spear?

Pamphilus. Not at all, but she's goddess of the sea.

Maria. I don't go sailing.

Pamphilus. But she has a boy.[3]

Maria. Boys don't scare me.

Pamphilus. He's vengeful and willful.

Maria. What will he do to me?

Pamphilus. What will he do? Heaven avert it! I wouldn't want to predict calamity to one whose welfare I have at heart.

Maria. Tell me anyway. I'm not superstitious.

Pamphilus. Then I'll tell you. If you reject this lover—who, unless I'm mistaken, is not altogether unworthy of having his love returned—the boy may, at his mother's bidding, shoot you with a dreadfully poisonous dart. As a result you'd fall desperately in love with some low creature who wouldn't return your love.

Maria. You tell me of a horrible punishment. For my part, I'd rather die than be madly in love with a man who's ugly or wouldn't return love for love.

2 Athenian court having special jurisdiction in cases of murder.
3 Cupid.

Pamphilus. Yet there was recently a much-publicized example of this misfortune, involving a certain girl.

Maria. Where?

Pamphilus. At Orleans.

Maria. How many years ago was this?

Pamphilus. How many years? Scarcely ten months ago.

Maria. What was the girl's name? Why do you hesitate?

Pamphilus. Never mind. I knew her as well as I do you.

Maria. Why don't you tell me her name, then?

Pamphilus. Because I don't like the omen. I only wish she'd had some other name! Hers was the very same as yours.

Maria. Who was her father?

Pamphilus. He's still living. Very eminent lawyer, and well-to-do.

Maria. Give me his name.

Pamphilus. Maurice.

Maria. Family name?

Pamphilus. Bright.

Maria. Is the mother living?

Pamphilus. Died recently.

Maria. What illness did she die of?

Pamphilus. What illness, you ask? Grief. And the father, though one of the hardiest of men, was in mortal danger.

Maria. May one know the mother's name too?

Pamphilus. Of course. Everybody knew Sophronia. But why this questioning? Do you think I'm spinning some yarn?

Maria. Would I suspect that of *you*? More commonly this suspicion is directed against our sex. But tell me what happened to the girl.

Pamphilus. She was a girl of respectable, wealthy background, as I said, and extremely beautiful; in short, worthy to marry a prince. She was courted by a certain young man whose social standing was similar to hers.

Maria. What was his name?

Pamphilus. Alas, a bad omen for me! Pamphilus was his name, too. He tried everything, but she obstinately turned him down. The young man wasted away with sorrow. Not so long afterwards she fell desperately in love with one who was more like an ape than a man.

Maria. What's that you say?

Pamphilus. So madly in love it's inexpressible.

Maria. So pretty a girl in love with so hideous a man?

Pamphilus. He had a peaked head, thin hair—and that torn and unkempt, full of scurf and lice eggs. The mange had laid bare most of his scalp; he was cross-eyed, had flat, wide-open nostrils like an ape's, thin mouth, rotten teeth, a stuttering tongue, pocky chin; he was hunchbacked, potbellied, and had crooked shanks.

Maria. You describe some Thersites [4] to me.

Pamphilus. What's more, they said he had only one ear.

Maria. Perhaps he lost the other in war.

Pamphilus. Oh, no, in peace.

Maria. Who dared do that to him?

Pamphilus. Denis the hangman.

Maria. Maybe a large family fortune made up for his ugliness.

Pamphilus. Not at all; he was bankrupt, and head over heels in debt. With this husband, so exceptional a girl now spends her life, and is often beaten.

Maria. A wretched tale you tell.

Pamphilus. But a true one. Thus it pleased Nemesis to avenge the injury to the youth who was spurned.

Maria. I'd rather be destroyed by a thunderbolt than put up with such a husband.

Pamphilus. Then don't provoke Nemesis: return your lover's love.

Maria. If that's enough, I do return it.

Pamphilus. But I'd want this love to be lasting, and to be mine alone. I'm courting a wife, not a mistress.

Maria. I know that, but I must deliberate a long time over what can't be revoked once it's begun.

Pamphilus. *I've* thought it over a very long time.

[4] In the *Iliad,* a slanderous Greek, "the ugliest man who came to Ilium" (ii, 216).

Maria. See that love, who's not the best adviser, doesn't trick you. For they say he's blind.

Pamphilus. But one who proceeds with caution is keen-sighted. You don't appear to me as you do because I love you; I love you because I've observed what you're like.

Maria. But you may not know me well enough. If you'd wear the shoe, you'd feel then where it pinched.

Pamphilus. I'll have to take the chance; though I infer from many signs that the match will succeed.

Maria. You're a soothsayer too?

Pamphilus. I am.

Maria. Then by what auguries do you infer this? Has the night owl [5] flown?

Pamphilus. That flies for fools.

Maria. Has a pair of doves [6] flown from the right?

Pamphilus. Nothing of the sort. But the integrity of your parents has been known to me for years now. In the first place, good birth is far from a bad sign. Nor am I unaware of the wholesome instruction and godly examples by which you've been reared; and good education is better than good birth. That's another sign. In addition, between my own line —not an altogether contemptible one, I believe—and yours there has long been intimate friendship. In fact, you and I have known each other to our fingertips, as they say, since childhood, and our temperaments are pretty much the same. We're nearly equal in age; our parents, in wealth, reputation, and rank. Finally—and this is the special mark of friendship, since excellence by itself is no guarantee of compatibility— your tastes seem to fit my character rather well. How my qualities agree with your character, I don't know. Obviously, darling, these omens assure me that we shall have a blessed, lasting, happy marriage, provided you don't intend to sing a song of woe for our prospects.

Maria. What song do you want?

[5] A lucky omen to the Athenians, since the owl was sacred to Pallas Athene.

[6] Sacred to Venus.

Pamphilus. I'll play "I am yours"; you chime in with "I am yours."

Maria. A short song, all right, but it has a long sequel.[7]

Pamphilus. What matter how long, if only it be joyful?

Maria. I think so highly of you that I wouldn't want you to do something you might later regret.

Pamphilus. Stop looking on the dark side.

Maria. Maybe I'll seem different to you when illness or old age has changed this beauty.

Pamphilus. Neither will I always be as handsome as I am now, my dear. But I don't consider only this dwelling place, which is blooming and charming in every respect. I love the guest more.

Maria. What guest?

Pamphilus. Your mind, whose beauty will forever increase with age.

Maria. Truly you're more than a Lynceus [8] if you see through so much make-up!

Pamphilus. I see your thought through mine. Besides, we'll renew our youth repeatedly in our children.

Maria. But meantime my virginity will be gone.

Pamphilus. True, but see here: if you had a fine orchard, would you want it never to bear anything but blossoms, or would you prefer, after the blossoms have fallen, to see the trees heavy with ripe fruit?

Maria. How artfully he argues!

Pamphilus. Answer this at least: which is the prettier

---

[7] Here, and on p. 35 ("But meanwhile speak just three words"), Maria has good reason to be wary of Pamphilus' plea to repeat the words "I am yours." In canon law such an exchange of vows in the present tense, whether made publicly or privately, could have been binding on both parties, constituting in effect a valid marriage which would thenceforth be unbreakable except for extraordinary reasons. Spousals *de futuro*, on the other hand, were engagements that could be broken. Maria is obviously receptive to Pamphilus' suit, but unwilling to bind herself by saying "I am yours."

[8] One of the Argonauts. He was so keen-sighted that he could see through the earth.

sight, a vine rotting on the ground, or encircling some post or elm tree and weighing it down with purple grapes?

Maria. You answer me in turn: which is the more pleasing sight, a rose gleaming white on its bush, or plucked and gradually withering?

Pamphilus. In my opinion the rose that withers in a man's hand, delighting his eyes and nostrils the while, is luckier than one that grows old on a bush. For that one too would wither sooner or later. In the same way, wine is better if drunk before it sours. But a girl's flower doesn't fade the instant she marries. On the contrary, I see many girls who before marriage were pale, run-down, and as good as gone. The sexual side of marriage brightened them so much that they began to bloom at last.

Maria. Yet virginity wins universal approval and applause.

Pamphilus. A maiden is something charming, but what's more naturally unnatural than an old maid? Unless your mother had been deflowered we wouldn't have this blossom here. But if, as I hope, our marriage will not be barren, we'll pay for one virgin with many.

Maria. But they say chastity is a thing most pleasing to God.

Pamphilus. And therefore I want to marry a chaste girl, that I may live chastely with her. It will be more a marriage of minds than of bodies. We'll reproduce for the State; we'll reproduce for Christ. By how little will this marriage fall short of virginity! And perhaps some day we'll live as Joseph and Mary did. But meantime we'll learn virginity; for one does not reach the summit all at once.

Maria. What's this I hear? Virginity to be violated in order to be learned?

Pamphilus. Why not? As by gradually drinking less and less wine we learn temperance. Which seems more temperate to you, the one who, sitting down in the midst of dainties, abstains from them, or the one secluded from those things that invite intemperance?

Maria. I think the man whom abundance cannot corrupt is more steadfastly temperate.

Pamphilus. Which more truly deserves praise for chastity, the man who castrates himself, or the one who, while sexually unimpaired, nevertheless abstains from sexual love?

Maria. My vote would go to the latter. The first I'd regard as mad.

Pamphilus. But don't those who renounce marriage by a strict vow castrate themselves, in a sense?

Maria. Apparently.

Pamphilus. Now to refrain from sexual intercourse isn't a virtue.

Maria. Isn't it?

Pamphilus. Look at it this way. If it were a virtue per se not to have intercourse, intercourse would be a vice. Now it happens that it *is* a vice *not* to have intercourse, a virtue to have it.

Maria. When does this "happen"?

Pamphilus. Whenever the husband seeks his due from his wife, especially if he seeks her embrace from a desire for children.

Maria. What if from lust? Isn't it right for him to be denied?

Pamphilus. It's right to reprove him, or rather to ask him politely to refrain. It's not right to refuse him flatly—though in this respect I hear few husbands complain of their wives.

Maria. But liberty is sweet.

Pamphilus. Virginity, on the other hand, is a heavy burden. I'll be your king, you my queen; we'll rule a family by our will. Or does this seem servitude to you?

Maria. The public calls marriage a halter.

Pamphilus. But those who call it that really deserve a halter themselves. Tell me, I beg you, isn't your soul imprisoned in your body?

Maria. Evidently.

Pamphilus. Like a little bird in a cage. And yet ask him

if he desires to be free. He'll say no, I think. Why? Because he's willingly confined.

Maria. Our fortune is modest.

Pamphilus. So much the safer. You'll increase it at home by thrift, which is not unreasonably called a large source of income; I'll increase it away from home by my industry.

Maria. Children bring countless cares with them.

Pamphilus. But they bring countless delights, and often repay the parents' devotion with interest many times over.

Maria. Loss of children is a miserable experience.

Pamphilus. Aren't you childless now? But why expect the worst in every uncertainty? Tell me, which would you prefer, never to be born or to be born to die?

Maria. Born to die, certainly.

Pamphilus. As those who have lived are more fortunate than those who never were born and never will be born, so the more miserable is childlessness, which never had and never will have offspring.

Maria. Who are these who are not and will not be?

Pamphilus. Although one who refuses to run the risks of human life—to which we are all, kings and commoners alike, equally liable—ought to give up life, still, whatever happens, you'll bear only half. I'll take over the larger share, so that if we have good luck the pleasure will be double; if bad, companionship will take away half the pain. As for me, if heaven summons, it will be sweet to die in your arms.

Maria. Men bear more readily what nature's universal laws decree. But I observe how much more distressed some parents are by their children's conduct than by their death.

Pamphilus. Preventing that is mostly up to us.

Maria. How so?

Pamphilus. Because, with respect to character, good children are usually born of good parents. Kites don't come from doves. We'll try, therefore, to be good ourselves. Next, we'll see that our children are imbued from birth with sacred teachings and beliefs. What the jar is filled with when new matters most.[9] In addition, we'll see that at home we provide an example of life for them to imitate.

Maria. What you describe is difficult.

Pamphilus. No wonder, because it's lovely. (And you're difficult too, for the same reason.) But we'll labor so much the harder to this end.

Maria. You'll have tractable material to work with. See that you form and fashion me.

Pamphilus. But meanwhile speak just three words.

Maria. Nothing easier, but once words have flown out they don't fly back. I'll give better advice for us both: confer with your parents and mine, to get the consent of both sides.

Pamphilus. You bid me woo, but in three words you can make success certain.

Maria. I don't know whether I could. I'm not a free agent. In former times marriages were arranged only by the elders' authority. But however that may be, I think our marriage will have more chance of success if it's arranged by our parents' authority. And it's your job to woo; that isn't appropriate to our sex. For we girls like to be swept off our feet, even if sometimes we're deeply in love.

Pamphilus. I won't be backward in wooing. Only don't let your decision alone defeat me.

Maria. It won't. Cheer up, Pamphilus dear.

Pamphilus. You're more strait-laced toward me in this business than I should like.

Maria. But first ponder your own private decision. Judge by your reason, not your feeling. What emotions decide is temporary; rational choices generally please forever.

Pamphilus. Indeed you philosophize very well, so I'm resolved to take your advice.

Maria. You won't regret it. But see here: a disturbing difficulty has turned up.

Pamphilus. Away with difficulties!

Maria. You wouldn't want me to marry a dead man?

[9] Horace, *Epistles,* I, ii, 69-70.

Pamphilus. By no means, but I'll revive.

Maria. You've removed the difficulty. Farewell, Pamphilus darling.

Pamphilus. That's up to you.

Maria. I bid you good night. Why do you sigh?

Pamphilus. "Good night," you say? If only you'd grant what you bid!

Maria. Don't be in too great a hurry. You're counting chickens before they're hatched.

Pamphilus. Shan't I have anything from you to take with me?

Maria. This scent ball, which may gladden your heart.

Pamphilus. Add a kiss at least.

Maria. I want to deliver to you a virginity whole and unimpaired.

Pamphilus. Does a kiss rob you of any of your virginity?

Maria. Then do you want me to bestow my kisses on others too?

Pamphilus. Of course not. I want your kisses kept for me.

Maria. I'll keep them for you. Though there's another reason why I wouldn't dare give away kisses just now.

Pamphilus. What's that?

Maria. You say your soul has passed almost entirely into my body, and that there's only the slightest particle left in yours. Hence I'm afraid this particle in you would skip over to me in a kiss, and you'd then become quite lifeless. So shake hands, a symbol of our mutual love; and farewell. Persevere in your efforts. Meanwhile I'll pray Christ to bless and prosper us both in what we do.

◄ IV ►

EXORCISM

First printed 1524. As an exposé of superstition this story is entertaining enough, but if Professor Preserved Smith's conjectures about some of the characters are correct, it has an additional interest. He suggested that Polus is John Colt, father-in-law of St. Thomas More; More himself would then be the tormented "spirit" (*A Key to the Colloquies of Erasmus*, 1927, pp. 31-32). Erasmus punned on "polus," "pullus," and "colt" in another colloquy also (see "A Pilgrimage for Religion's Sake," p. 82). The identifications cannot be proved, but they are convincing. More's love of fun and of acting parts is well attested by his friends and biographers.

The colloquy is somewhat confusing because it mentions three persons of the same name: Faunus the father-in-law of Polus, Faunus the exorcist, and Faunus the "spirit," son-in-law of Polus. In Roman religion, Faunus or Fatuus was the name of an oracular god, identified with Pan. Erasmus' use of the name is perhaps due to the similarity between Fatuus and *fatuus*, "fool."

To Erasmus, as to More, "Exorcism" would have recalled some of the tales of their favorite Lucian, whose *Philopseudes*—a satire of human credulity—More had translated.

THOMAS, ANSELM

Thomas. What's the good news that makes you chuckle so merrily, as if you had stumbled on a treasure?

Anselm. Your guess is not far from the mark.

Thomas. But you'll let an old friend in on your good luck, won't you?

Anselm. Oh yes, I've been hoping for a long time to run across someone to share the fun with.

Thomas. Come on, then; out with it.

Anselm. I've just heard the most delightful story. You'd

swear it was a comic fiction, if I weren't as familiar with the setting, the characters, and the whole affair as I am with you.

Thomas. I can't wait to hear it.

Anselm. You know Polus, Faunus' son-in-law, don't you?

Thomas. Certainly.

Anselm. He's the author of this play as well as an actor in it.

Thomas. I'd readily believe it, for even without a mask he could act out any play.

Anselm. So he could. You know, too, I suppose, the estate that he has not far from London.

Thomas. Why, of course. We've drunk together there many a time.

Anselm. Then you know the road lined on each side by trees planted at regular intervals.

Thomas. To the left of the buildings, about two bow-shots off.

Anselm. Correct. Along one side of the road is a dry ditch grown over with briers and brambles. From the little bridge a path leads to the open field.

Thomas. I remember.

Anselm. Long ago a rumor spread among the peasants in the neighborhood that a specter of some sort had been seen near this little bridge, and its woeful howlings were heard repeatedly. They took it for the soul of someone suffering frightful torments.

Thomas. Who started the rumor?

Anselm. Who but Polus? He had made it up as a prologue to his play.

Thomas. What put it into his head to invent these things?

Anselm. I don't know, except that the man is naturally fond of playing tricks on people's stupidity by devices of this kind. I'll tell you what he recently contrived in this vein. A large company of us—including some you'd call sober, sensible men—were riding to Richmond. The sky was marvelously clear, unobscured by the slightest bit of cloud anywhere. Thereupon Polus, staring at the sky, crossed himself with a sweeping gesture and, with a look of blank astonishment, muttered as though to himself, "Good God, what do I see?" When those who were riding beside him asked him what he saw, he said (crossing himself again even more sweepingly), "May the most merciful God avert this portent!" While they pressed him, impatient in their curiosity, he kept his eyes fixed on the heavens, and, pointing with his finger to a region of the sky, "Don't you see," he said, "the huge dragon there, armed with fiery horns, its tail twisted into a circle?" When they insisted they did not see it, and he had ordered them to look hard and pointed out the place again and again, someone or other, anxious not to seem unobservant, finally declared that he too saw it. One after another followed suit, for they were ashamed not to see what was so perfectly clear! Why go on? Within three days, report of the appearance of such a portent had spread throughout England. But it's wonderful how much the story grew in the telling. Some persons, in all seriousness, expounded the meaning of the wonder. The man who had set the story going thoroughly enjoyed their folly.

Thomas. I know his character. But get back to the apparition.

Anselm. Meanwhile Polus found his chance, thanks to Faunus, a parish priest in the vicinity—one of the sort who aren't satisfied with the Latin name of regulars unless they're equipped with the same title in Greek.[1] He looked upon himself as uncommonly wise, especially in divinity.

Thomas. I see: an actor for the play was found.

Anselm. At dinner, conversation turned to the report about the specter. When Polus noticed that Faunus not only had heard this story but believed it too, he began to beseech this learned and reverend man to rescue the poor soul who was suffering such awful torments. "And if you have any doubts," he says, "investigate the matter for yourself. Walk by that little bridge at ten o'clock and you'll hear the wretched wailing. Take with you any companion you like, so as to hear with more safety and certainty."

[1] I.e., canons. See "A Pilgrimage for Religion's Sake," p. 63.

Thomas. Then what?

Anselm. After dinner Polus, according to his custom, went hunting or fowling. Faunus, strolling about when the shadows had already made it impossible to be sure of one's judgment of objects, finally heard the miserable groans. Polus—who's a remarkably clever fellow—was making them from his hiding place there in the brier patch, with the help of an empty earthenware jar to make his voice sound the more mournful.

Thomas. This play, I see, beats Menander's *Specter.*[2]

Anselm. You'll go further than that if you hear the whole story. Faunus went back home, eager to relate what he had heard. Polus, taking a short cut, had already arrived. There Faunus tells him what happened, and he even embroiders the tale to make it more impressive.

Thomas. How could Polus keep from laughing all the while?

Anselm. He? Oh, he has perfect control of his expression. You'd have said some serious topic was under discussion. At last, on Polus' earnest entreaty, Faunus undertook the task of exorcism, and stayed up all that night pondering ways and means of tackling the job safely, since he was terribly frightened on his own account too. First the most effective exorcisms were collected, and some new ones added: "by the bowels of the Blessed Mary," "by the bones of Blessed Winifred."[3] Next a spot was chosen in the field adjoining the brier patch from which the voice was heard, and a circle, large enough to hold the numerous crucifixes and the various signs, marked off. All of this was executed with the proper ritual. A large vessel filled with holy water was brought. In addition, a sacred stole (as it's called), with the opening verses of St. John's Gospel hanging from it, was draped over Faunus' shoulders. In his pockets he had a waxen image of the kind blessed annually by the pope and known as an Agnus Dei. Long ago—before a Franciscan cowl became so formidable—people used to protect themselves by this armor against harmful demons.

[2] Only fragments of this comedy survive.
[3] Welsh saint (seventh century), credited with many miracles.

All this equipment was provided in the event that the spirit proved to be an evil one and attacked the exorcist. Still, Faunus didn't dare trust himself to the circle alone. It was decided that a second priest should be present. Then Polus, afraid that if a smarter one were added the secret of the play would be discovered, brought a certain parish priest from the neighborhood. To him he divulged the whole plot, because acting out the play necessitated this, and the priest was one who would enjoy this sort of joke. About ten o'clock the following night, when everything had been duly prepared, Faunus and the parish priest entered the circle. Polus, who has gone on ahead, groans woefully from the brier patch. Faunus commences the exorcism. Meantime Polus sneaks off secretly through the shadows to a cottage nearby, whence he brings another actor for the play; for the performance required a large cast.

Thomas. What do they do?

Anselm. Mount black horses and carry concealed fire with them. When they're near the circle they display the fire, to scare Faunus out of the circle.

Thomas. What a lot of trouble Polus took to play a trick!

Anselm. That's the sort of man he is. But this business almost ended in disaster for them.

Thomas. How so?

Anselm. Because the horses took fright at the fire that was suddenly produced and almost upset both themselves and their riders. There you have Act I of the play. When the subject came up for discussion again, Polus, as though ignorant of it all, asks what happened. Faunus then tells of seeing two most dreadful devils on black horses, with blazing eyes, and breathing fire from their nostrils. They attempted to enter the circle, he said, but were dispatched to hell by his potent spells. Full of confidence after this, Faunus returned to the circle next day with all his trappings. When he had called up the specter, after many long-winded invocations, Polus and his partner again showed themselves from a distance on their black horses, roaring frightfully as if they wanted to break into the circle.

Thomas. Had they no fire?

Anselm. None, for that strategem hadn't turned out well. But listen to this other device. They brought with them a long rope. Skipping it along the ground while they each rushed hither and yon as though driven by Faunus' exorcisms, they tumbled both priests to the ground, and the jar of holy water as well.

Thomas. Did the priest put up with this kind of payment for his acting?

Anselm. He did, and preferred to endure this rather than give up his role. After all this, when they talked about the matter again, Faunus proclaimed in Polus' presence what a narrow escape he'd had, and how boldly he'd overcome each devil with his spells. And by this time he was absolutely convinced that there was no demon so harmful or brazen that it could break into the circle.

Thomas. That Faunus was not far from being a fool.[4]

Anselm. You've heard nothing yet. When the play had reached this point, Polus' son-in-law (husband of his eldest daughter) opportunely intervened. He is, as you know, a young man with a wonderful sense of humor.

Thomas. I know. He's not averse to pranks of this kind.

Anselm. Averse? He'd jump bail set at any sum if a play like this were to be seen or acted. His father-in-law unfolds the whole story, and designates him to play the part of the spirit. He dons a costume, and very willingly, too: wraps himself in a linen sheet, as we wrap corpses. In a jug he has a live coal which looks like fire when seen through the linen. At nightfall they go to the scene of the play. Wondrous groans are heard. Faunus sets off all his exorcisms. At last the spirit discloses itself from some distance away in the brier patch, showing the fire repeatedly and sighing miserably. When

[4] "Necromancers put their trust in their circles, within which they think themself sure against all the devils in hell" (More, *Dialogue Concerning Tyndale*, I, iii; *English Works*, ed. W. E. Campbell and A. W. Reed, 1931ff., II, 25).

Faunus conjured it to tell who it was, Polus, dressed like a devil, suddenly jumped up from the brier patch and roared, "You have no right to this soul. It's mine!" and rushed to the edge of the circle again and again, as if he were going to attack the exorcist. Soon he retreated, as though driven back by the words of the exorcism and the power of the holy water that Faunus doused him with liberally. At last, after the head devil's departure, Faunus and the spirit begin a conversation. To Faunus' pressing inquiries, the spirit replies that it is the soul of a Christian. Asked its name, it answers "Faunus." "Faunus!" says the other, "Why, that's my name." Now, because of their common name, he becomes very eager for Faunus to free Faunus.

Although Faunus kept asking about many other matters, the soul withdrew, lest a long-drawn-out conversation give the trick away. He swore he was forbidden to talk any longer, saying that the hour was come when he was forced to go wherever the devil pleased. Nevertheless he promised to return next day at the time permitted.

Once more there was a reunion at the house of Polus, the director of this play. There the exorcist gave an account of what happened. He garnished the story with some fictions that he was convinced were facts, so much was he enjoying the affair. Already it was certain that the soul was a Christian one, subjected to dreadful tortures by a merciless devil. Faunus' efforts were directed wholly to this problem. But at the very next exorcism a ridiculous thing occurred.

Thomas. What, I beg you?

Anselm. After Faunus had called up the spirit, Polus, who played the devil, rushed forward as if he were going to break into the circle. When Faunus opposed this with exorcisms and sprinkled a lot of holy water on him, the devil finally cried that he cared not a straw for all that. "You've had dealings with a girl," he said. "You're mine by rights." Polus said this as a joke, but evidently he chanced to hit upon the truth, for the exorcist was silenced by this utterance and withdrew to the center of the circle and whispered something or other to the priest. Observing this, Polus fell back to avoid overhearing what was unlawful to hear.

Thomas. Clearly Polus behaved like a reverent and modest devil!

Anselm. So he did. Otherwise his conduct might have been blamed as most improper. Still, he did overhear the voice of the priest imposing penance.

Thomas. What was it?

Anselm. That Faunus should say the Lord's Prayer three times. From this Polus guessed that he had had relations with the girl three times in the same night.

Thomas. That Regular broke the regulations, all right.

Anselm. They're men, and to err is human.

Thomas. Go on: what happened next?

Anselm. Faunus, now sterner than ever, returns to the edge of the circle and willingly calls up the devil. But he, more hesitant now, shrank back, saying, "You deceived me; had I known, I would not have reminded you." Many folk are convinced that what you've once confessed to a priest is immediately wiped from the devil's remembrance, so he may not reproach you.

Thomas. That's a very silly joke you're telling.

Anselm. But—to finish the story at last—conversation with the spirit continued in this manner for some days. The upshot was this: when the exorcist asked whether there was no way of freeing the soul from torment, it replied yes, this could be done if restitution were made of the money it had left— money got by fraud. Thereupon Faunus says, "What if it were spent by good men for pious purposes?" He answered that this would be satisfactory. Delighted with this, the exorcist inquired very carefully how large the sum was. "A very big one," was the reply, which was good, comforting news to Faunus. The spirit also informed him of where this treasure was buried (a place far away) and gave explicit directions about the purposes for which it was to be spent.

Thomas. What purposes were they?

Anselm. It was to enable three men to make pilgrimages. One of them was to go to the threshold of Peter; the second was to salute James of Compostella; [5] the third was to kiss the comb of Jesus at Trier.[6] Next, a great number of psalms and masses was to be performed by some monasteries. The remainder was to be spent as he thought best. By this time Faunus' mind was entirely on the treasure. He had swallowed it whole.

Thomas. It's a common weakness, although priests have a particularly bad reputation in this respect.

Anselm. When nothing remained to be settled concerning money matters, the exorcist, on a hint from Polus, began to ask the spirit about occult arts, alchemy, and magic. And to these questions the soul replied for the time being, but promised to relate much more as soon as the exorcist's labor had freed it from the devil its master. Let this be, if you like, Act III of the play.

In Act IV, Faunus began to proclaim everywhere, in dead earnest, the prodigious thing that had happened. In conversations and at dinners he prattled of nothing else; he promised splendid gifts to monasteries; and his talk now had no modesty whatever about it. He went to the place and found the signs, but still he didn't dare dig up the treasure, because the soul had put an obstacle in his way: namely, that it would be extremely dangerous to touch the treasure before the masses were performed. By this time the trick was suspected by many of the shrewder sort. Yet when he never for one moment stopped making a fool of himself everywhere, he was warned confidentially by his friends, especially by his abbot, to beware lest one who had heretofore been considered a man of sound judgment should now show himself to the world an example of something quite different. But he could not be moved by any plea to take the matter less seriously. So thoroughly did this fancy obsess him that he dreamt of noth-

[5] See the opening of "A Pilgrimage for Religion's Sake."

[6] The most famous relic there was the Holy Coat, which tradition declared to be the seamless garment of Christ (see John 19:23-24).

ing but specters and evil spirits, and he talked of nothing else. His mental condition carried over into his very countenance, which became so pale, so drawn, so downcast that you would have said he was a ghost, not a man. What more need I say? He would have been close to real insanity had not relief come through a quick cure.

Thomas. This will surely be the final act of the play.

Anselm. I'll tell you about it. Polus and his son-in-law contrived a trick, of this sort: they devised a letter written in an unusual script, and not on ordinary paper but the kind goldsmiths coat with gold leaf—reddish-brown, as you know. Its sense was: "Faunus, long captive now free, to Faunus his most excellent liberator, perpetual greeting. You have no reason, my dear Faunus, to torment yourself further in this affair. God has regarded the righteous intention of your heart, and as a reward has freed me from torture. Now I live in bliss with the angels. There is a place awaiting you beside St. Augustine, next to the choir of Apostles. When you come to us, I shall thank you in front of them all. Meantime see that you live a happy life. Given from the empyrean heaven on the Ides of September, 1498, under seal of my ring." This letter was placed secretly on the altar where Faunus was to officiate. After this someone was instigated to tip him off about the thing, as though the letter had been discovered by accident. Faunus now carries the letter round and displays it as if it were something sacred; and he believes nothing more firmly than that it was brought from heaven by an angel.

Thomas. This wasn't freeing a man from insanity but changing the brand of insanity!

Anselm. Very true, except that now he's mad in a more pleasant way.

Thomas. Up to this time I haven't, as a rule, put much faith in popular tales about apparitions, but hereafter I'll be far more skeptical. For I suspect that many pieces of writing put out by credulous men like Faunus were faked by some such trick.

Anselm. I, too, believe that most of them are of this kind.

∞∫∮ V ∮∫∞

ALCHEMY

First published 1524. Perhaps the best-known story of alchemy and alchemists between *The Canon's Yeoman's Tale* of Chaucer and Jonson's *The Alchemist*. It may have con-. tributed something to Jonson's comedy. A translation of this colloquy appears in Reginald Scott's once-important *Discovery of Witchcraft* (1584), Book XIV, chapter 5.

"Philecous" means "fond of listening"; "Lalus" means "talkative."

PHILECOUS, LALUS

Philecous. What's happened to amuse Lalus so? He's nearly bursting with laughter, and he crosses himself again and again. I'll interrupt the man's bliss.—Greetings, my dear Lalus! You seem very happy.

Lalus. But I'll be happier if I share this pleasure with you.

Philecous. Then do me the favor as soon as you can.

Lalus. You know Balbinus? [1]

Philecous. That learned, much-esteemed gentleman?

Lalus. Just as you say, but no mortal is wise at all times, or perfect in every respect. Along with many brilliant gifts, the gentleman has this slight blemish: that for a long while he's been mad about the art called alchemy.

Philecous. What you refer to is not a blemish, surely, but a notorious disease.

Lalus. However that may be, Balbinus, often as he's been taken in by this class of men, nevertheless allowed himself to be marvelously cheated a little while ago.

Philecous. How?

---

[1] The name is probably borrowed from Horace, whose Balbinus is blind to the defects of his mistress (*Sat.*, I, iii, 40).

Lalus. A certain priest came to him, greeted him deferentially, and soon began thus: "Most learned Balbinus, you wonder perhaps why an ignorant creature like me should interrupt you in this fashion, when I know you never rest a moment from your most sacred studies." Balbinus nodded, as is his custom, for he's remarkably sparing of words.

Philecous. That's proof of shrewdness.

Lalus. But the other, who was shrewder, continued: "Yet you'll forgive this impertinence of mine when you learn my reason for coming to you." "Tell it," says Balbinus, "but in few words if possible." "I'll tell it as briefly as I can," says he. "You know, most learned of men, that mortals have different destinies. I'm uncertain whether to include myself among the happy or the unhappy. For if I consider my fate from one standpoint, I think I'm very lucky; but if from another, no one seems less lucky than I." When Balbinus urged him to cut it short, "I'll finish, most learned Balbinus," he says. "It will be all the easier for me to address a man whose knowledge of this whole business is unexcelled."

Philecous. You're describing a rhetorician to me, not an alchemist.

Lalus. You'll hear the alchemist in a moment. "From boyhood," he says, "I've had the good fortune to learn by far the most eagerly sought of all arts, that core of all philosophy, I say—alchemy." At the word "alchemy" Balbinus started somewhat—a mere gesture—but uttering a groan, bade him continue. Then says the other, "But O wretched me! I did not follow the right path." When Balbinus asked him what paths he was talking about, he replied, "You know, Excellency—for what escapes you, Balbinus, a man most learned in every respect?—that there is a twofold path in this art: one named longation, the other curtation. But I had the misfortune to fall into longation." When Balbinus inquired what the difference was between the two ways, he replied, "It's presumptuous of me to speak of these matters in your presence when I know that your familiarity with them is unsurpassed. And so I've hurried here to you in hopes that you might take pity on me and deign to share with me that most blessed way of curtation. The more learned you are in this science, the less trouble it will be for you to impart it to me. Do not conceal so great a gift of God from a brother who is about to die of grief. So may Jesus Christ ever enrich you with greater gifts!"

Since he made no end of entreaties, Balbinus was forced to confess that he simply didn't know what longation or curtation was. He bids the man explain the meaning of these terms. Then says the other, "Although I know I'm talking to a man of superior learning, nevertheless I'll do as you command. Those who have spent an entire lifetime on this sacred science transmute species of things by two methods. One is shorter but a little more risky; the other takes longer but is safer. I regard myself as unlucky: up to now I've toiled in this latter path, which does not please me, and I've been unable to find anyone willing to show me the other path that I'm dying to find. At last God put it into my mind to come to you, a man as good as you are learned. Knowledge enables you to grant my request without trouble; goodness will move you to take compassion on a brother whose welfare is in your power."

In brief, after the sly old rascal, by this kind of talk, had dispelled suspicion of fraud and had convinced Balbinus of his perfect understanding of the other way, Balbinus was already itching with impatience. Finally, unable to restrain himself, he says, "Away with that curtation! I've never even heard of it, let alone mastered it. Tell me straight, do you understand longation well?" "Pooh!" says the other, "To a T. But the length I don't care for." When Balbinus asked him how much time it took, he replied, "Too much—almost a whole year. It's the safest way, though." "Don't worry even if the job takes two years," says Balbinus, "provided you're sure of your skill." To make a long story short, they reach an agreement to undertake the business secretly in Balbinus' house, on condition that the priest do the work and Balbinus put up the money. The profit was to be divided half and half, although the swindler—modest fellow!—voluntarily assigned all anticipated profit to Balbinus. And each swears an oath of secrecy, like persons initiated into secret rites. Money is counted out then and there for the operator to buy pots, glasses, charcoal, and other equipment needed for the laboratory. This money our alchemist promptly and enjoyably squanders on whores, dice, and drink.

Philecous. That's changing the species of things, all right!

Lalus. To Balbinus' urging that they get to work, he replied, "Don't you agree with the saying that 'Well begun is half done'? It's a big job to prepare the material properly." At last he began fitting up the furnace. Here again more gold was needed: a lure to catch later gold, as it were. As a fish isn't landed without bait, so an alchemist produces no gold unless he has some to begin with.

Meanwhile Balbinus devoted all his time to calculations. He was figuring how much profit, if one ounce yielded fifteen, would be made from two thousand ounces; for so much had he determined to invest. After the alchemist had run through this money, too, and already had pretended for a month or so to be busy with bellows and charcoal, Balbinus asked him how the work was coming along. At first he was silent. Finally, when Balbinus pressed him, he answered, "Just as important projects generally come along—they're always hard to get under way." He gave as the reason a mistake in buying charcoal: he had bought some made from oak when fir or hazel was required. There went a hundred gold crowns—and the dice went rolling just as promptly!

With the new grant of money the charcoal was replaced. Now the work was started more earnestly than before: as, in a war, if soldiers suffer a setback, they make up for it by valor. When the laboratory [2] had glowed for some months now, and the golden fruit was expected, and not a bit of gold was left in the vessels (for by this time the alchemist had squandered all that too), another excuse was alleged: the glasses used had not been heated properly. For as a likeness of Mercury isn't fashioned from just any kind of wood, so gold isn't made in

[2] See the drawing, "The Alchemist's Household," by Brueghel the Elder.

glasses of just any kind. The greater the investment, the slighter was the inclination to give up.

Philecous. That's like gamblers. As if it weren't much better to cut your losses than to lose everything!

Lalus. So it is. The alchemist swore he'd never been so cheated. Now that the error was corrected, the rest would be quite safe, and this loss would be made good, with a large amount of interest besides.

After the glasses were changed, the laboratory was set up for the third time. The alchemist suggested that their business would succeed better if he sent some gold crowns as an offering to the Virgin Mother who, as you know, is worshiped at Paralia.[3] For the art is a sacred one, and cannot prosper without the blessing of heaven. This advice was most acceptable to Balbinus, since he was a devout man who would not let a day go by without attending divine service. The alchemist set out on his pious journey—to the next village, that is, and there spent the votive money in riotous living. Home again, he announces he has the highest hopes that their enterprise will prosper in accordance with their wishes, so pleased did the Holy Virgin seem with his offering.

When, after much time and toil, not even a grain of gold had been produced, the alchemist, in reply to Balbinus' complaint, declared he had never had such an experience in his life, expert though he was in this art: he couldn't guess what the trouble was. Finally, after much pondering, it occurred to Balbinus to wonder if the alchemist had missed hearing mass on any day, or failed to say his rosary, as they call it; for nothing succeeds if these are neglected. Thereupon the swindler replies, "You've hit the nail on the head. Wretched me! I did forget to do that once or twice, and lately I forgot to salute the Virgin on rising from a long-drawn-out dinner

[3] *Paraliis.* The meaning of the word is uncertain. If it is intended to be a form of *paralius,* "by the sea," it may refer to Walsingham. In "A Pilgrimage for Religion's Sake," Erasmus refers to Our Lady of Walsingham as *Virginem Parathalassiam.*

party." "No wonder," says Balbinus then, "that so important a matter doesn't succeed." The expert undertook to hear twelve masses for the two he had missed, and in place of a single salutation to make ten.

When the spendthrift alchemist had gone broke time after time, and no excuses for demanding money presented themselves, he finally thought up this trick. He arrived home out of breath and moaned, "I'm done for, Balbinus, done for; I'll swing for this!" Balbinus was amazed and impatient to learn the cause of so great a disaster. "Some officials at court got word of what we're up to," he says, "and I fully expect to be dragged off to jail any minute." At this speech Balbinus turned pale in earnest, for you know that to practice alchemy without royal permission is a capital crime in these parts. The other continues, "I'm not afraid of death; I only hope that's what I get. I'm afraid of something more cruel." To the question of what this was, he answers, "That I'll be carried off to a tower somewhere and forced to slave there all my life for persons against my will. Is there any death not preferable to such a life?"

Then and there they examined the matter from every angle. Balbinus, since he was a master of rhetoric, hammered away at every position,[4] seeking an escape from the danger. "Can't you deny the crime?" he says. "By no means," says the other. "The affair is common knowledge among the king's men, and they have evidence that can't be brushed aside." So plain was the law that they could put up no defense. After many possibilities had been weighed and nothing very reassuring appeared, the alchemist, who was now sorely in need of cash, finally said, "Balbinus, we take our time discussing it, but the problem demands an immediate solution. I think they're coming very soon to arrest me." In the end, when Balbinus could think of nothing by way of reply, the alchemist said, "I can't think of anything either, nor do I see anything left to do except die bravely. Unless, perhaps, this one remaining possibility appeals to you. It's a useful rather than honor-

[4] *Status:* a technical term in law.

able one, except that necessity is a cruel goad. You know," says he, "that men of this sort are greedy of money, and therefore it's rather easy to bribe them to keep their mouths shut. However hard it may be to give those rascals money to throw away, still, as things now stand, I see no better remedy." Balbinus agreed, and counted out thirty gold crowns to stop their tongues.

Philecous. That's wonderful generosity on Balbinus' part.

Lalus. Oh, no; in any honest business you would sooner have drawn a tooth from him than a farthing. Thus the alchemist was provided for. He was in no danger except that of having no money to give to his mistress.

Philecous. I'm surprised Balbinus wasn't alert in such an important matter.

Lalus. Only in this is he gullible. In others he's extremely alert. With fresh funds the furnace was set up once more, but first brief prayers were made to the Virgin Mother, to win her favor for the undertaking. Already a whole year had passed, while the alchemist made up one excuse after another; the labor was lost and the investment wasted. Meantime an absurd accident occurred.

Philecous. What was it?

Lalus. The alchemist was having a secret affair with the wife of a courtier. Her husband, his suspicions aroused, began to keep an eye on the man. At last, when he was informed that the priest was in the bedroom, he returned home unexpectedly and pounded on the door.

Philecous. What was he going to do to the fellow?

Lalus. What? Nothing pleasant—either kill him or castrate him. When the husband, insistent, threatened to break down the door if his wife didn't open it, a great commotion resulted. Some instant remedy was sought. There was none but that offered by the situation itself. The man threw off his cloak, lowered himself through a narrow window—not without risk or injury—and fled. Such stories get around quickly, you know. So the word reached Balbinus too, as the alchemist foresaw it would.

Philecous. And thus he's caught in the middle.

Lalus. On the contrary, he got out of this more luckily than from the bedroom. Mark the fellow's trick. Balbinus did not protest, but showed well enough by his stern expression that he was not unaware of the gossip. The alchemist knew that Balbinus was strait-laced—I might almost say superstitious—in some things. Such men readily forgive an offender, no matter how serious his fault. So the other purposely brings up the success of the business. He complains that he's not getting along as well as usual, or as he would like, adding emphatically that he wonders what the reason is. Balbinus, who otherwise seemed resolved upon silence, was aroused at once by this opportunity; and he was a man easily aroused. "There's no mystery about what the trouble is," he says. "Your sins block the success of what should be handled by pure men in a pure way." At this word the alchemist dropped to his knees, beating his breast repeatedly, and with tearful looks and tone said, "Balbinus, you've spoken the absolute truth. My sins, I admit, are the hindrance. But they're my sins, not yours, for I shan't be ashamed to confess my disgrace before you, as before the holiest priest. Weakness of the flesh overcame me; Satan drew me into his snares, and—O wretched me!—from priest I am become an adulterer. Yet the offering we made to the Virgin Mother was not altogether wasted. I would certainly have been killed if she had not come to my rescue. The husband was breaking down the door; the window was too narrow for me to slip through. In so imminent a danger I thought of the Most Holy Virgin. I fell on my knees and implored her, if the gift had been acceptable, to help me. Without further delay I tried the window again—my plight forced me to do so —and found it was wide enough for my escape." [5]

Philecous. Balbinus believed this?

Lalus. Believed it? More than that, he forgave him, and piously warned him not to show himself ungrateful to the Most Blessed Virgin. Once more money was paid out to the

[5] See the story in "A Pilgrimage for Religion's Sake," pp. 65-66.

alchemist, who promised that hereafter his conduct in this solemn business would be above reproach.

Philecous. How did it turn out?

Lalus. It's a long story, but I'll finish it in few words. After he had made a fool of the man for a long time by tricks of this sort, and fleeced him of no mean sum of money, the affair finally came to the ears of one who had known the rascal from boyhood. Readily guessing that the fellow was doing the same thing in Balbinus' house that he had done everywhere, he visits Balbinus secretly, explains what kind of "expert" he shelters in his house, and warns him to get rid of the man as quickly as possible unless he wants that same expert to make off sometime after robbing Balbinus' desk.

Philecous. What did Balbinus do at this? He had him thrown into jail, surely?

Lalus. Jail? Oh, no: he gave him travel money, imploring him by everything sacred not to blab about what had happened. And in my opinion he was wise to prefer this to having the story become the talk of the town, and, in the second place, to risking confiscation of his property. The impostor was in no danger. He understood the "art" about as well as an ass does, and in an affair of this kind swindling is regarded leniently. Besides, if he had attempted robbery, benefit of clergy would have saved him from hanging. Nor would anyone willingly be at the expense of keeping him in jail.

Philecous. I might feel sorry for Balbinus if he himself didn't enjoy being gulled.

Lalus. I must hurry to court now. Some other time I'll tell you far more foolish tales.

Philecous. I'll be glad to hear them when I have time, and I'll match you story for story.

✒ VI ᕥ

A PILGRIMAGE FOR RELIGION'S SAKE

First printed 1526. This famous colloquy grew out of visits made by Erasmus to the shrines of Our Lady of Walsingham (1512 and possibly again in 1514) and St. Thomas of Canterbury (*c.* 1514), the two most popular places of pilgrimage in England. For light on these shrines in his time, and on his account of them, the reader may consult the notes to J. G. Nichols' translation of the colloquy (second edition, 1875), C. E. Woodruff and W. Danks' *Memorials of the Cathedral and Priory of Christ in Canterbury* (1912), and J. C. Dickinson's *The Shrine of Our Lady of Walsingham* (1956). Mr. Dickinson argues that Erasmus' report of what he saw and heard at Walsingham is far from reliable. Undoubtedly his strong opinions about pilgrimages, plus his desire to tell a good story, made him a prejudiced witness. We should remember, however, that he did not (presumably) write the colloquy until long after his visit. In the meantime he may simply have forgotten some things.

"Menedemus" means "stay-at-home." "Ogygius" may be coined from the name Ogygia, a western island mentioned in the *Odyssey;* or it may stand for "Boeotian," i.e., "simpleminded," "stupid" (Ogygius was the mythical founder of Thebes in Boeotia).

When, a decade after publication of this colloquy, the government of Henry VIII began to suppress the English monasteries, destroy the shrines, and confiscate their treasures, an anonymous translation of Erasmus' dialogue appeared under the title *The Pilgrimage of Pure Devotion*. It is scarcely likely that a work so useful as propaganda would have been permitted to come out at just this time had not Thomas Cromwell or his agents been interested in seeing it published.

MENEDEMUS, OGYGIUS

Menedemus. What marvel is this? Don't I see my neighbor Ogygius, whom nobody's laid eyes on for six whole months? I heard he was dead. It's his very self, unless I'm los-

56

ing my mind completely. I'll go up to him and say hello.
—Greetings, Ogygius!

Ogygius. Same to you, Menedemus.

Menedemus. Where in the world do you turn up from, safe and sound? A sad rumor spread here that you'd sailed in Stygian waters.

Ogygius. No, thank heaven; I've seldom enjoyed better health.

Menedemus. I hope you'll always be able to refute silly rumors of that sort! But what's this fancy outfit? You're ringed with scallop shells, choked with tin and leaden images on every side, decked out with straw necklaces, and you have snake eggs on your arms.[1]

Ogygius. I've been on a visit to St. James of Compostella and, on my way back, to the famous Virgin-by-the-Sea, in England;[2] or rather I revisited her, since I had gone there three years earlier.

Menedemus. Out of curiosity, I dare say.

Ogygius. Oh, no: out of devotion.

Menedemus. Greek letters, I suppose, taught you that devotion.

Ogygius. My wife's mother had bound herself by a vow that if her daughter gave birth to a boy and he lived, I would promptly pay my respects to St. James and thank him in person.

Menedemus. Did you greet the saint only in your own name and your mother-in-law's?

Ogygius. Oh, no, in the whole family's.

Menedemus. Well, I imagine your family would have been no less safe even if you had left James ungreeted. But do please tell me: what answer did he make when you thanked him?

---

[1] Shells, traditional symbols of pilgrims, were connected especially with St. James and the pilgrimage to Compostella. The "snake eggs" are beads, i.e., a rosary.

[2] Two celebrated shrines, one in northwestern Spain, the other at Walsingham, Norfolk.

Ogygius. None, but he seemed to smile as I offered my gift, nodded his head slightly, and at the same time held out these scallop shells.

Menedemus. Why does he give these rather than something else?

Ogygius. Because he has plenty of them; the sea nearby supplies them.

Menedemus. O generous saint, who both delivers those in labor and gives presents to callers! But what new kind of vowing is this, that some lazy person lays the work on others? If you bound yourself by a vow that, should *your* affairs prosper, *I* would fast twice a week, do you think I'd do what you had vowed?

Ogygius. No, I don't, even if you'd sworn in your own name. For you enjoy mocking the saints. But she's my mother-in-law; custom had to be kept. You're acquainted with women's whims, and besides I had an interest in it, too.

Menedemus. If you hadn't kept her vow, what risk would there have been?

Ogygius. The saint couldn't have sued me at law, I admit, but he could have been deaf thereafter to my prayers, or secretly have brought some disaster upon my family. You know the ways of the mighty.

Menedemus. Tell me, how is the excellent James?

Ogygius. Much colder than usual.

Menedemus. Why? Old age?

Ogygius. Joker! You know saints don't grow old. But this newfangled notion that pervades the whole world results in his being greeted more seldom than usual. And if people do come, they merely greet him; they make no offering at all, or only a very slight one, declaring it would be better to contribute that money to the poor.

Menedemus. An impious notion!

Ogygius. And thus so great an Apostle, accustomed to shine from head to foot in gold and jewels, now stands a wooden figure with hardly a tallow candle to his name.

Menedemus. If what I hear is true, there's danger that other saints may come to the same pass.

Ogygius. More than that: a letter is going round which the Virgin Mary herself wrote on this very theme.

Menedemus. Which Mary?

Ogygius. The one called Mary a Lapide.

Menedemus. At Basel,[3] unless I'm mistaken.

Ogygius. Yes.

Menedemus. Then it's a stony saint you tell me of. But to whom did she write?

Ogygius. She herself gives the name in the letter.

Menedemus. Who delivered the letter?

Ogygius. Undoubtedly an angel, who placed it on the pulpit from which the recipient preaches. And to prevent suspicion of fraud, you shall see the very autograph.

Menedemus. So you recognize the hand of the angel who is the Virgin's secretary?

Ogygius. Why, of course.

Menedemus. By what mark?

Ogygius. I've read Bede's epitaph,[4] which was engraved by an angel. The shape of the letters agrees entirely. Also I've read the manuscript message to St. Giles.[5] They agree. Aren't these facts proof enough?

Menedemus. Is one allowed to see it?

Ogygius. Yes, if you'll promise to keep your mouth shut about it.

Menedemus. Oh, to tell me is to tell a stone.

[3] Mariastein, near Basel. A statue of the Virgin there was famous for its miracles.

[4] In the abbey church at Durham. The word *venerabilis* was said to have been added to Bede's epitaph by the hand of an angel.

[5] Legend said that when St. Giles interceded with God for the remission of the king's sins, an angel appeared and placed on the altar a scroll which announced that the sins were forgiven. The story is in the *Golden Legend* (September 1). In some versions Giles is confused with other saints of the same name, and the king is sometimes said to have been Charles Martel, sometimes Charlemagne.

Ogygius. But some stones [6] are notorious for giving secrets away.

Menedemus. Then tell it to a deaf man, if you don't trust
a stone.

Ogygius. On that condition I'll read it. Lend me your
ears.

Menedemus. I've lent them.

Ogygius. "Mary, Mother of Jesus, to Glaucoplutus: [7]
greetings. Know that I am deeply grateful to you, a follower
of Luther, for busily persuading people that the invocation of
saints is useless. For up to this time I was all but exhausted
by the shameless entreaties of mortals. They demanded everything from me alone, as if my Son were always a baby (because he is carved and painted as such at my bosom), still
needing his mother's consent and not daring to deny a person's prayer; fearful, that is, that if he did deny the petitioner
something, I for my part would refuse him the breast when
he was thirsty. And sometimes they ask of a Virgin what a
modest youth would hardly dare ask of a bawd—things I'm
ashamed to put into words. Sometimes a merchant, off for
Spain to make a fortune, commits to me the chastity of his
mistress. And a nun who has thrown off her veil and is preparing to run away entrusts me with her reputation for virtue—which she herself intends to sell. A profane soldier, hired
to butcher people, cries upon me, 'Blessed Virgin, give me
rich booty.' A gambler cries, 'Help me, blessed saint; I'll share
my winnings with you!' And if they lose at dice, they abuse
me outrageously and curse me, because I wouldn't favor their
wickedness. A woman who abandons herself to a life of shame
cries, 'Give me a fat income!' If I refuse anything, they protest at once, 'Then you're no mother of mercy.'

6 Touchstones, which tell whether supposed gold is true or not (Pliny,
Natural History, XXXIII, xliii, 126).

7 "Owl-rich," a play on the first name of Ulrich Zwingli, the Swiss
Reformer. When this letter was censured by the Sorbonne, Erasmus
replied that it was directed against the Zwinglians (*Opera Omnia*, Leiden
edition, IX, 948E).

"Some people's prayers are not so irreverent as absurd. An unmarried girl cries, 'Mary, give me a rich and handsome bridegroom.' A married one, 'Give me fine children.' A pregnant woman, 'Give me an easy delivery.' An old woman, 'Give me a long life without a cough or a thirst.' A doddering old man, 'Let me grow young again.' A philosopher, 'Give me power to contrive insoluble problems.' A priest, 'Give me a rich benefice.' A bishop, 'Preserve my church.' A sailor, 'Give me prosperous sailings.' A governor, 'Show me thy Son before I die.' A courtier, 'Grant that at point of death I may confess sincerely.' A countryman, 'Give me a heavy rain.' A country woman, 'Save the flock and herd from harm.' If I deny anything, straightway I'm cruel. If I refer to my Son, I hear, 'He wills whatever you will.' So am I alone, a woman and a virgin, to assist those who are sailing, fighting, trading, dicing, marrying, bearing children; to assist governors, kings, and farmers?

"What I've described is very little in comparison with what I endure. But nowadays I'm troubled much less by these matters. For this reason I would give you my heartiest thanks, did not this advantage bring a greater disadvantage along with it. I have more peace, but less honor and wealth. Formerly, I was hailed as 'Queen of Heaven, mistress of the world'; now I hear scarcely an 'Ave Maria' even from a few. Formerly I was clothed in gold and jewels; I had many changes of dress; I had golden and jeweled offerings made to me. Now I have hardly half a cloak to wear, and that one is mouse-eaten. My annual income is scarcely enough to keep the wretched sacristan who lights the little lamp or tallow candle. And yet all these hardships I could have borne, if you weren't said to be plotting even greater ones. You're trying, they say, to remove from the churches whatever belongs to the saints. Now just consider what you're doing. Other saints have means of avenging injuries. If Peter is ejected from a church, he can in turn shut the gate of heaven against you. Paul has a sword; Bartholomew is armed with a knife. Under his monk's robe

William [8] is completely armed, nor does he lack a heavy lance. And what could you do against George, with his horse and his coat of mail, his spear and his terrible sword? Anthony's not defenseless, either: he has his sacred fire.[9] Others likewise have weapons or mischiefs they direct against anybody they please. But me, however defenseless, you shall not eject unless at the same time you eject my Son whom I hold in my arms. From him I will not be parted. Either you expel him along with me, or you leave us both here, unless you prefer to have a church without Christ. I wanted you to know this. Think carefully what to answer, for my mind's absolutely made up. From our stony house, on the Calends of August, in the year of my Son's passion 1524. I, the Virgin a Lapide, have signed this with my own hand."

Menedemus. A dreadful, threatening letter, indeed! I imagine Glaucoplutus will take warning.

Ogygius. If he's wise.

Menedemus. Why didn't the excellent James write to him on this same subject?

Ogygius. I don't know, except that he's rather far away, and all letters are intercepted nowadays.

Menedemus. But what fortune brought you back to England?

Ogygius. An unexpectedly favorable breeze carried me there, and I had virtually promised the saint-by-the-sea that I would pay her another visit in two years.

Menedemus. What were you going to ask of her?

Ogygius. Nothing new, just the usual things: family safe and sound, a larger fortune, a long and happy life in this world, and eternal bliss in the next.

Menedemus. Couldn't the Virgin Mother here at home see to those matters? At Antwerp she has a church much grander than the one by the sea.

Ogygius. I can't deny that, but different things are be-

---

[8] St. William of Gellone, called Duke of Aquitaine. As a soldier in the service of Charlemagne, he fought against the Saracens.

[9] Erysipelas.

stowed in different places, either because she prefers this or (since she is obliging) because she accommodates herself in this respect to our feelings.

Menedemus. I've often heard about James, but I beg you to describe for me the domain of the Virgin-by-the-Sea.

Ogygius. Well, I'll do the best I can in brief. She has the greatest fame throughout England, nor would you readily find anyone in that island who hoped for prosperity unless he greeted her annually with a small gift, according to his means.

Menedemus. Where does she live?

Ogygius. By the northwest [10] coast of England, only about three miles from the sea. The village has scarcely any means of support apart from the tourist trade. There's a college of canons, to whom, however, the Latins add the title of regulars: an order midway between monks and the canons called seculars.[11]

Menedemus. You're telling me of amphibians, such as the beaver.

Ogygius. Yes, and the crocodile. But details aside, I'll try to satisfy you in a few words. In unfavorable matters they're canons; in favorable ones, monks.

Menedemus. So far you're telling me a riddle.

Ogygius. But I'll add a precise illustration. If the Roman pontiff assailed all monks with a thunderbolt, then they'd be canons, not monks. Yet if he permitted all monks to take wives, then they'd be monks.

Menedemus. Strange favors! I wish they'd take mine too.

Ogygius. But to get to the point. This college depends almost entirely on the Virgin's generosity for its support. The larger gifts are kept, to be sure, but any small change, anything of trifling value, goes towards the support of the community and their head, whom they call the prior.

Menedemus. Do they live holy lives?

Ogygius. They're not unpraised. They're richer in piety

[10] A slip; Walsingham is in northern Norfolk.

[11] They were Austin canons. Erasmus himself was a member of this order.

than income. The church is fine and splendid, but the Virgin doesn't dwell there; in honor of her Son she yields that to him. She has her own church, that she may be to the right of her Son.

Menedemus. The right? Which direction does the Son face, then?

Ogygius. I'm glad you remind me. When he faces west he has his mother on his right; when he turns to the east she's on his left. However, she doesn't dwell here, either, for the building is not yet finished, and the place is quite airy—windows and doors open, and Ocean, father of the winds, nearby.

Menedemus. Too bad. So where does she live?

Ogygius. In that church, which as I said is unfinished, is a small chapel built on a wooden platform. Visitors are admitted through a narrow door on each side. There's very little light: only what comes from tapers, which have a most pleasing scent.

Menedemus. All this is appropriate to religion.

Ogygius. Yes, and if you peered inside, Menedemus, you would say it was the abode of the saints, so dazzling is it with jewels, gold, and silver.

Menedemus. You make me impatient to go there.

Ogygius. You wouldn't regret the trip.

Menedemus. Is there no holy oil there?

Ogygius. Silly! That oil exudes only from the tombs of saints, such as Andrew and Catherine. Mary isn't buried.

Menedemus. My mistake, I admit. But finish your story.

Ogygius. As the cult spreads more widely, different things are displayed in different places.

Menedemus. In order, perhaps, that the giving may be more generous; as it is said, "Loot quickly comes when sought by many hands." [12]

Ogygius. And custodians are always present.

Menedemus. Some of the canons?

Ogygius. No, they're not used, lest on a favorable opportunity for religious devotion they might stray from devout-

[12] Ovid, *Amores*, I, viii, 92.

ness, and while honoring the Virgin pay too little regard to their own virginity. Only in the interior chapel, which I said is the inner sanctum of the Holy Virgin, a canon stands by the altar.

Menedemus. What for?

Ogygius. To receive and keep the offering.

Menedemus. Do people contribute whether they want to or not?

Ogygius. Not at all, but a sort of reverent shame impels some to give when a person's standing by. They wouldn't give if no one were present to watch them. Or sometimes they give more generously than they would otherwise.

Menedemus. That's human nature. I'm no stranger to it.

Ogygius. Nay, there are some so devoted to the Most Holy Virgin that while they pretend to lay an offering on the altar, they steal, with astonishing nimbleness, what somebody else had placed there.

Menedemus. Suppose there's no witness: would the Virgin strike them dead on the spot?

Ogygius. Why would the Virgin do that, any more than does the heavenly Father himself, whom men aren't afraid to rob of treasures, even digging through the church wall for the purpose?

Menedemus. I can't tell which to be the more astonished at, their impious audacity or God's mildness.

Ogygius. Then, on the north side—not of the church (don't mistake me) but of the wall enclosing the whole area adjacent to the church—is a certain gateway. It has a tiny door, the kind noblemen's gates have, so that whoever wants to enter must first expose his shins to danger and then stoop besides.

Menedemus. Certainly it wouldn't be safe to go at an enemy through such a door.

Ogygius. Right. The custodian told me that once a knight on horseback escaped through this door from the hands of an enemy who was on the point of overtaking him in his flight. In despair he commended himself then and there to the Holy Virgin, who was close by. For he had determined to take refuge at her altar if the door was open. And mark this wonder: suddenly the knight was entirely within the churchyard and the other man outside, furious.

Menedemus. And was this wondrous tale of his believed?

Ogygius. Of course.

Menedemus. A philosophical chap like you wouldn't accept it so easily.

Ogygius. He showed me on the door a copper plate, fastened by nails, containing a likeness of the knight who was saved, dressed in the English fashion of that period as we see it in old pictures—and if pictures don't lie, barbers had a hard time in those days, and so did weavers and dyers.

Menedemus. How so?

Ogygius. Because the knight was bearded like a goat, and his clothing didn't have a single pleat, and was so tight it made the body itself thinner. There was another plate, too, showing the size and shape of the shrine.

Menedemus. You no longer had any reason to doubt!

Ogygius. Beneath the little door was an iron grating, admitting you only on foot. It was not seemly that a horse should afterwards trample the spot the horseman had consecrated to the Virgin.

Menedemus. And quite rightly.

Ogygius. To the east is a small chapel, filled with marvels. I betake myself to it. Another custodian receives us. After we've prayed briefly, we're immediately shown the joint of a human finger (the largest of three). I kiss it and then ask whose relics these are. "Saint Peter's," he says. "Not the Apostle Peter's?" "Yes." Then, looking at the great size of the joint, which might have been a giant's, I said, "Peter must have been an extremely big man." At this one of my companions burst into a loud laugh, which annoyed me no end, for if he had been quiet the attendant would have kept none of the relics from our inspection. However, we appeased him with some coins.

In front of the little building was a structure that during the wintertime (he said), when everything was covered by snow, had been brought there suddenly from far away.[13] Under this were two wells, filled to the top. They say the stream of water is sacred to the Holy Virgin. It's a wonderfully cold fluid, good for headache and stomach troubles.

Menedemus. If cold water cures headache and stomach troubles, oil will put out fire next.

Ogygius. You're hearing about a miracle, my good friend —besides, what would be miraculous about cold water quenching thirst?

Menedemus. Clearly this is only one part of the story.

Ogygius. That stream of water, they declared, suddenly shot up from the ground at the command of the Most Holy Virgin. Inspecting everything carefully, I inquired how many years it was since the little house had been brought there. "Some ages," he replied. "In any event," I said, "the walls don't look very old." He didn't dissent. "Even these wooden posts don't look old." He didn't deny they had been placed there recently, and the fact was self-evident. "Then," I said, "the roof and thatch of the house seem rather recent." He agreed. "Not even these crossbeams, nor the very rafters supporting the roof, appear to have been put here many years ago." He nodded. "But since no part of the building has survived, how is it known for certain," I asked, "that this *is* the cottage brought here from so far away?"

Menedemus. How did the attendant get out of that tangle, if you please?

[13] The "little building" must be the chapel mentioned in the preceding paragraph (i.e., the chapel of St. Laurence, east of the church; see J. C. Dickinson, *The Shrine of Our Lady of Walsingham*, 1956, pp. 91-106 and plates 3b, 4b). The "structure . . . brought there suddenly from far away" seems to be a reference to another chapel, the Holy House, which contained the famous statue of Our Lady. This chapel was supposedly a copy of the house in Nazareth in which Mary received the Annunciation. (The original house at Nazareth, according to a late medieval legend, was miraculously transported to Loretto, in Italy, where it became a favorite resort of pilgrims.) There was a story that while the Holy House was being built east of the church, angels moved it 200 feet to the north side. Erasmus perhaps confuses this story with the wilder one about the Santa Casa of Loretto. See Dickinson, *op. cit.*, pp. 55, 91-106.

Ogygius. Why, he hurriedly showed us an old, worn-out bearskin fastened to posts, and almost laughed at us for our dullness in being slow to see such a clear proof. So, being persuaded, and excusing our stupidity, we turned to the heavenly milk of the Blessed Virgin.

Menedemus. O Mother most like her Son! He left us so much of his blood on earth; she left so much of her milk that it's scarcely credible a woman with only one child could have so much, even if the child had drunk none of it.

Ogygius. The same thing is said about the Lord's Cross, which is exhibited publicly and privately in so many places that if the fragments were joined together they'd seem a full load for a freighter. And yet the Lord carried his whole cross.

Menedemus. Doesn't it seem amazing to you, too?

Ogygius. It could be called unusual, perhaps, but "amazing"—no, since the Lord, who multiplies these things as he wills, is omnipotent.

Menedemus. You explain it reverently, but for my part I'm afraid many such affairs are contrived for profit.

Ogygius. I don't think God will stand for anybody mocking him in that way.

Menedemus. On the contrary, although Mother and Son and Father and Spirit are robbed by the sacrilegious, sometimes they don't even bestir themselves slightly enough to frighten off the criminals by a nod or a noise. So great is the mildness of divinity.

Ogygius. That's true. But hear the rest. This milk is kept on the high altar, in the midst of which is Christ; on the right, for the sake of honor, is his mother. For the milk represents his Mother.

Menedemus. So it's in plain sight.

Ogygius. Enclosed in crystal, that is.

Menedemus. Therefore liquid.

Ogygius. What do you mean, liquid, when it flowed fifteen hundred years ago? It's hard: you'd say powdered chalk, tempered with white of egg.

Menedemus. Why don't they display it exposed?

Ogygius. To save the virginal milk from being defiled by the kisses of men.

Menedemus. Well said, for in my opinion there are those who would bring neither clean nor chaste mouths to it.

Ogygius. When the custodian saw us, he rushed up to it, donned a linen vestment, threw a sacred stole round his neck, prostrated himself devoutly, and adored. Soon afterward he held out the sacred milk for us to kiss. We prostrated ourselves devoutly on the lowest step of the altar and, after first saluting Christ, uttered to the Virgin a short prayer I had prepared for this occasion: "Virgin Mother, who hast had the honor of suckling at thy maidenly breast the Lord of heaven and earth, thy Son Jesus, we pray that, cleansed by his blood, we may gain that blessed infancy of dovelike simplicity which, innocent of all malice, deceit, and guile, longs without ceasing for the milk of gospel doctrine until it attains to the perfect man, to the measure of the fullness of Christ, whose blessed company thou enjoyest forever, with the Father and Holy Spirit. Amen."

Menedemus. Certainly a devout intercession. What effect did it have?

Ogygius. Mother and Son both seemed to nod approval, unless my eyes deceived me. For the sacred milk appeared to leap up, and the Eucharistic elements gleamed somewhat more brightly. Meanwhile the custodian approached us, quite silent, but holding out a board [14] like those used in Germany by toll collectors on bridges.

Menedemus. Yes, I've often cursed those greedy boards when traveling through Germany.

Ogygius. We gave him some coins, which he offered to the Virgin. Next, through an interpreter who understands the language well (a smooth-tongued young man named Robert Aldridge,[15] I believe), I tried as civilly as I could to find out what proof he had that this *was* the Virgin's milk. I wanted

[14] Or "box."

[15] A Cambridge scholar who worked with Erasmus. Later Provost of Eton and Bishop of Carlisle.

to know this clearly for the pious purpose of stopping the mouths of certain unbelievers who are accustomed to laugh at all these matters. At first the custodian frowned and said nothing. I told the interpreter to press him, but even more politely. He did so with the utmost grace, such that if with words of that sort he had entreated the Mother herself, recently out of childbed, she would not have taken offense. But the custodian, as if possessed, gazed at us in astonishment, and as though horrified by such a blasphemous speech, said, "What need is there to inquire into that when you have an authentic record?" And it looked very much as if he would throw us out for heretics, had we not calmed the fellow's wrath with money.

Menedemus. What did you do then?

Ogygius. What do you suppose we did? As though beaten with a club, or struck by a thunderbolt, we took ourselves out of there, humbly begging pardon (as one should in sacred matters) for such outrageous presumption. Then on to the little chapel, the shrine of the Holy Virgin. At our approach a custodian turns up, a Minorite, and gazes at us, as though studying us; after we go a little farther a second one turns up, likewise staring at us; then a third.

Menedemus. Perhaps they wanted to draw you.

Ogygius. But I suspected something very different.

Menedemus. What was that?

Ogygius. That a sacrilegious person had filched something from the Holy Virgin's ornaments, and that their suspicion was directed against me. So when I entered the chapel I greeted the Virgin Mother with a short prayer, like this: "O thou alone of all womankind Mother and Virgin, Mother most blessed, purest of maidens, we who are unclean come unto thee who art pure. We bless thee, we worship thee as best we can with our poor gifts. May thy Son grant us that, by emulating thy most blessed life, we too, through the grace of the Holy Spirit, may be made worthy to conceive the Lord Jesus spiritually in our inmost hearts, and never lose him once conceived. Amen." Kissing the altar at the same time, I laid some coins upon it and went away.

Menedemus. What did the Virgin do at this? Didn't she indicate by the slightest nod that your short prayer was heard?

Ogygius. As I told you, there was a dim religious light, and she stood in the shadows, to the right of the altar. Finally, the first custodian's harangue had so squelched me that I didn't dare lift my eyes.

Menedemus. So this expedition didn't end very happily.

Ogygius. On the contrary, quite happily.

Menedemus. You've brought me back to life, for "my heart had fallen to my knees," [16] as your Homer says.

Ogygius. After lunch we went back to the church.

Menedemus. You dared to, when you were suspected of sacrilege?

Ogygius. That may be, but I was not suspect in my own eyes. A good conscience knows no fear. I wanted to see the "record" to which the guide had referred us. After searching for it a long time, we found it, but the board was hung so high nobody could possibly read it. I'm no Lynceus [17] so far as eyes are concerned, nor am I totally blind, either. So as Aldridge read, I followed along, not trusting him completely in so vital a matter.

Menedemus. Were all your doubts cleared up?

Ogygius. I was ashamed of having doubted, so clearly was the whole thing set forth before my eyes—the name, the place, the story, told in order. In a word, nothing was omitted. There was said to be a certain William of Paris, a holy man, inasmuch as from time to time he was remarkably devoted to searching the world over for saints' relics. After traveling through many lands, visiting monasteries and churches everywhere, he came at length to Constantinople, where his brother was bishop. When William was preparing to return, his brother confided to him that a certain nun had the milk of the Virgin Mother, and that he would be extremely blessed

16 *Iliad*, xv, 280.
17 Proverbially keen-sighted Argonaut.

ever afterwards if by prayer, purchase, or artifice he could get hold of a portion of it. For all other relics he had collected to date were as nothing compared with this sacred milk. From that moment William could not rest until by his begging he won a little of the milk. With this treasure he thought himself richer than Croesus.

Menedemus. Why not? And beyond expectation, too.

Ogygius. He hurried straight home, but a fatal illness stopped him short.

Menedemus. How slight, brief, and limited is human happiness!

Ogygius. Aware of the danger, he summons a fellow pilgrim, a most reliable Frenchman. Swearing him to secrecy, he entrusts the milk to him on condition that if he reaches home safely he is to place this treasure on the altar of the Holy Virgin who dwells in the great church in Paris, overlooking the Seine that flows by on each side—the river itself seems to give way in honor of the Virgin's sanctity. To make a long story short, William is buried; the other hurries on; and disease takes him, too. In despair of his life, he gives the milk to an English companion, but binds him by many oaths to do what he himself had intended to do. He dies; the other takes the milk and places it on the altar in the presence of the canons there (formerly called regulars, as they are yet at St. Genevieve's). From them he begged a little of the milk. This he carried to England and finally brought to St. Mary-by-the-Sea, summoned to this place by divine inspiration.

Menedemus. Surely this story is very consistent.

Ogygius. More than that: lest any uncertainty remain, there were inscribed, above, the names of suffragan bishops who grant indulgences as extensive as their supply affords to those who come to see the milk and don't neglect to leave a small offering.

Menedemus. How much can they grant?

Ogygius. Forty days.

Menedemus. Are there days even in the underworld?

Ogygius. There's time, certainly.

Menedemus. When the whole supply's been granted, is there none left to give out?

Ogygius. On the contrary: what they grant is inexhaustible. And obviously this is different from what happens to the jar of the Danaides, since that, although continuously filled, is always empty; but as for this, if you always drain it, you still have no less in the jar.

Menedemus. If forty days apiece are granted to a hundred thousand men, each man has so much?

Ogygius. Yes.

Menedemus. And if those who received forty days before lunch were to ask for the same number again at dinnertime, it would be at hand to bestow?

Ogygius. Oh, yes, even if they asked for it ten times an hour.

Menedemus. Wish I had such a money box at home! I'd ask merely for three drachmas if only they renewed themselves.

Ogygius. If the answer to your prayer is to be so large as that, you're hoping to turn into gold completely. But to resume the story. This "proof" was added, with pious simplicity: that although the Virgin's milk shown in a great many other places was of course to be reverenced, nevertheless this was to be venerated more than that elsewhere, because that was scraped from rocks whereas this flowed from the Virgin's own breasts.

Menedemus. How was this known?

Ogygius. Oh, the nun of Constantinople, who gave the milk, said so.

Menedemus. And perhaps St. Bernard informed her?

Ogygius. That's what I think.

Menedemus. The one who in old age was privileged to taste milk from that same breast which the child Jesus sucked. Hence I'm surprised he's called "the mellifluous" instead of "the lactifluous." But how can that be called the Virgin's milk which did not flow from her breasts?

Ogygius. It did flow, but falling on the rock where she

happened to be sitting when giving suck, it hardened and then, by God's will, so increased.

Menedemus. Right. Continue.

Ogygius. After this, while we're strolling about, looking at sights of interest before departing, the custodians turn up again, glance at us, point with the finger, run up, go away, rush back, nod; they seemed to be on the point of accosting us if they could find courage enough.

Menedemus. Weren't you at all scared then?

Ogygius. Oh, no, I looked them straight in the eye, smiling and gazing at them as if inviting them to address me. At last one comes near and asks my name. I give it. He asks if I was the man who two years earlier had put up a votive tablet in Hebrew.[18] I admit it.

Menedemus. Do you write Hebrew?

Ogygius. Of course not, but anything they don't understand they call Hebrew. Soon the protos-hysteros of the college comes—having been sent for, I imagine.

Menedemus. What title is that? Don't they have an abbot?

Ogygius. No.

Menedemus. Why?

Ogygius. Because they don't know Hebrew.[19]

Menedemus. Nor a bishop?

Ogygius. No.

Menedemus. Why?

Ogygius. Because the Virgin is still too hard up to buy an expensive staff and miter.

Menedemus. Don't they have at least a provost?

Ogygius. Not even that.

Menedemus. Why not?

Ogygius. Because "provost" is a title designating office, not sanctity. And that's why colleges of canons reject the name of "abbot." That of "prior" they accept willingly.

Menedemus. But "protos-hysteros" I never heard of before.

18 Erasmus did compose a Greek poem to the Virgin of Walsingham.
19 "Abbot" is from Syriac, which Ogygius apparently takes for Hebrew.

Ogygius. Really, you're very ignorant of grammar.

Menedemus. I do know "hysteron proteron" in figures of speech.

Ogygius. Exactly. The man next to the prior is posterior-prior.

Menedemus. You mean a *sub*prior.

Ogygius. This man greeted me decently enough. He tells me how hard many persons toil to read those lines, and how often they wipe their spectacles in vain. Whenever some aged D.D. or J.D. came along he was marched off to the tablet. One would say the letters were Arabic; another, that they were fictitious characters. Finally one was found who could read the title. It was written in Roman words and letters, but in capitals. The Greek lines were written in Greek capitals, which at first glance look like Latin capitals. Upon request, I gave the meaning of the verses in Latin, translating word for word. I refused the small tip proffered for this bit of work, declaring there was nothing, however difficult, that I would not be very eager to do for the sake of the Most Holy Virgin, even if she bade me carry a letter from there to Jerusalem.

Menedemus. Why would she need you as postman when she has so many angels to wait on her hand and foot?

Ogygius. He offered from his bag a piece of wood, cut from a beam on which the Virgin Mother was seen to stand. A marvelous fragrance proved at once that the object was an extremely sacred one. After kissing so remarkable a gift three or four times with the utmost devotion, while prone and bareheaded, I put it in my purse.

Menedemus. May one see it?

Ogygius. I'll let you see it. But if you aren't fasting, or if you had intercourse with your wife last night, I shouldn't advise you to look at it.

Menedemus. No danger. Show it to me.

Ogygius. Here you are.

Menedemus. Oh, how lucky you are to have this present!

Ogygius. In case you don't know, I wouldn't **exchange**

this tiny fragment for all the gold in Tagus.[20] I'll set it in gold, but so that it shines through crystal.

Then Hystero-protus, when he saw that I was so reverently delighted with this little gift, and decided I was not undeserving of having greater matters entrusted to me as well, asked whether I had ever seen the secrets of the Virgin. This word startled me somewhat, but I didn't dare ask which secrets of the Virgin he meant, since in subjects so sacred even a slip of the tongue can be dangerous. I say I haven't seen them, but that I want to very much. I'm led on now as though divinely inspired. One or two wax tapers are lighted, and a small image displayed, unimpressive in size, material, and workmanship, but of surpassing power.

Menedemus. Size has little to do with producing miracles. I've seen the Christopher at Paris,[21] not merely of wagon or colossus size but fully as big as a mountain—yet he was distinguished for no miracles that I ever heard of.

Ogygius. At the Virgin's feet is a jewel, as yet unnamed by Latins or Greeks. The French have named it from "toad," [22] because it shows the figure of a toad in a way no art could achieve. What's more wonderful, the stone is very small; the image of the toad does not stick out but shines through in the jewel itself, as if inlaid.

Menedemus. Perhaps they imagine the toad's likeness, as we imagine an eagle in a stalk of fern. And similarly, what don't children see in clouds: dragons breathing fire, mountains burning, armed men clashing.

Ogygius. For your information, no toad shows itself more obviously alive than that one did.

Menedemus. So far I've put up with your stories. From now on, look for someone else to convince with your toad yarn.

Ogygius. No wonder you feel like that, Menedemus. No-

[20] River in Spain and Portugal.

[21] A statue formerly in the Church of Notre Dame. See "The Shipwreck," p. 7.

[22] The crapaud stone or bufonite.

body could have persuaded me either, even if the whole
Faculty of Theology had maintained it, unless I had seen it,
inspected it, and made certain of it with these eyes—these very
eyes, I tell you. But you do strike me as rather lacking in
curiosity about natural history.

Menedemus. Why? Because I don't believe asses fly?

Ogygius. Don't you see how Nature the artist enjoys expressing herself in the colors and forms of everything, but
especially in jewels? Then, how marvelous the powers she put
into those jewels: well-nigh incredible, did not firsthand ex-
experience give us assurance of them. Tell me, would you have
believed steel is pulled by a magnet without being touched,
and repelled by it again without contact, unless you had seen
it with your own eyes?

Menedemus. No, never, even if ten Aristotles had sworn
it to me.

Ogygius. Then don't cry "Incredible!" as soon as you hear
about something not yet known by experience. In *ceraunia*
we see the figure of a thunderbolt; in *pyropus,* living fire; in
chalazias, the appearance and hardness of hail, even if you
throw it into the midst of the fire; in the emerald, deep, clear
sea water. *Carcinias* resembles a sea crab; adderstone, a viper;
scarites, the fish called scarus; *hieracites,* a falcon. *Geranites*
has a neck like the crane's; *aegophthalmus,* a goat's eye (one
kind shows a pig's eye, another three human eyes together);
lycophthalmus paints the eye of a wolf in four colors: golden
red, blood red, and in the middle black bordered by white.
If you open *cyamea nigra,* you'll find a bean in the center.
Dryites looks like a tree trunk and burns like wood. *Cissites*
and *narcissites* depict ivy; *astrapias* throws out flashes of
lightning from its white or lapis-lazuli center; *phlegontes*
shows inside the color of flame, which does not die out; in the
coal carbuncle you see certain sparks darting; *crocias* has the
color of a crocus; *rhodites,* of a rose; *chalcites,* of brass. Eagle-
stone represents an eagle, with a whitish tail; *taos* has the
image of a peacock; swallowstone, that of an adder. *Myrme-
cites* contains the figure of a creeping ant; *cantharias* shows a

complete beetle; *scorpites* illustrates a scorpion remarkably.[23] But why pursue these examples, which are countless, since nature has no part—in the elements, in living things, or in plants—that it does not illustrate, as if in sport, in precious stones. Do you wonder that a toad is imaged in this jewel?

Menedemus. I wonder that Nature has so much leisure to play thus at imitating everything.

Ogygius. She wanted to arouse the curiosity of mankind, and so to shake us out of our idleness. And yet—as though we had no way of escaping boredom!—we go crazy over jesters, dice, and jugglers' tricks.

Menedemus. Very true.

Ogygius. Some sober people say that if stones of this kind are put in vinegar, the "toads" will move their legs and swim.

Menedemus. Why is the toad set before the Virgin?

Ogygius. Because she overcame, stamped out, extinguished all impurity, infection, pride, avarice, and whatever earthly passions there are.

Menedemus. Woe to us who bear so great a toad in our breasts!

Ogygius. We shall be pure if we worship the Virgin zealously.

Menedemus. How does she like to be worshiped?

Ogygius. You will adore her most acceptably if you imitate her.

Menedemus. Precisely—but that's very hard to do.

Ogygius. Yes, but most glorious.

Menedemus. Go on; continue what you began.

Ogygius. Next he shows us gold and silver statues. "This one," says he, "is all gold; the other one, silver gilded." He adds the weight and worth of each, and the name of the donor. When, marveling at every one, I was congratulating

[23] Since identification of many of these stones is uncertain, their classical names are kept in the translation. Erasmus borrowed the list from Pliny's *Natural History*, XXXVII, xi, 72-73. Erasmus wrote some notes to a 1516 edition of Pliny, and a preface to a 1525 edition.

the Virgin on such fortunate wealth, the guide said: "Since I notice you're a devout sightseer, I don't think it right to keep anything from you: you shall see the Virgin's very greatest secrets." At the same time he takes down from the altar itself a world of wonderful things. If I tried to enumerate them all, the day would not be long enough. Thus the pilgrimage ended very happily for me. I had my fill of sights, and I brought away with me this priceless gift, a pledge from the Virgin herself.

Menedemus. Didn't you test the power of your piece of wood?

Ogygius. I did. Before three days passed, I found at a certain inn a man who had gone mad; they were ready to chain him. I slipped this wood under his pillow secretly. He fell into a long, deep sleep. In the morning he woke up as sound as ever.

Menedemus. Maybe it wasn't insanity but delirium tremens from drink. Sleep usually helps that malady.

Ogygius. Joke as you please, Menedemus, but about something else. To make fun of the saints is neither reverent nor prudent. Why, the man himself said that a woman of marvelous beauty had appeared to him in a dream and held out a cup to him.

Menedemus. Hellebore, I dare say.

Ogygius. I don't know about that, but I *do* know the man's in his right mind.

Menedemus. Did you overlook Thomas, Archbishop of Canterbury?

Ogygius. By no means. No pilgrimage is more devout.

Menedemus. I long to hear about it, if that's not too much trouble.

Ogygius. Oh, no, I want you to hear. There's a section of England called Kent, facing France and Flanders. Its chief city is Canterbury. In it are two monasteries, almost adjacent, both of them Benedictine houses. That named for St. Augustine is evidently the older; the one now called after St.

Thomas [24] appears to have been the Archbishop's seat, where he used to live with a few chosen monks; just as today, too, bishops have residences adjoining the churches but apart from the houses of other canons. (In old time both bishops and canons were usually monks; evidence abounds to prove that.) The church sacred to St. Thomas rises to the sky so majestically that it inspires devotion even in those who see it from afar. Thus by its splendor it now dims the glory of the neighboring one and, so to speak, overshadows the spot that was anciently the most sacred. It has two huge towers, as though greeting visitors a long way off and making the region ring far and wide with the wonderful sound of its bronze bells. At the south entrance of the church are stone statues of three armed men, who with sacrilegious hands murdered the blessed saint. Their surnames are added: Tusci, Fusci, Berri.[25]

Menedemus. Why is so much honor paid to impious men?

Ogygius. Obviously they have the same honor as Judas, Pilate, and Caiaphas, that band of wicked soldiers whom you see carefully carved on gilded altars. The surnames are added lest anybody in the future speak well of them. Attention is called to them in order that hereafter no courtier lift a hand against bishops or Church property. For those three conspirators went mad after committing their crime, and would not have recovered had they not begged help of the most holy Thomas.

Menedemus. O the everlasting mercy of martyrs!

Ogygius. When you enter, the spacious grandeur of the building is disclosed. This part is open to the public.

Menedemus. Is there nothing to see there?

Ogygius. Nothing but the mass of the structure, and some books—among them the Gospel of Nicodemus—fastened to pillars, and a tomb, I don't know whose.[26]

---

[24] "That named for St. Augustine": formerly the abbey of SS. Peter and Paul; "the one now called after St. Thomas": the priory of Christ Church.

[25] William de Tracy, Reginald Fitzurse, and Richard le Breton or Brito. Erasmus omits the name of the fourth, Hugh de Morville.

[26] The tombs of two archbishops, Islip and Whittlesey.

Menedemus. Then what?

Ogygius. Iron screens prevent you from going any farther, but they permit a view of the space between the end of the building and the choir, as it is called. This is ascended by many steps, under which a certain vault [27] gives access to the north side. A wooden altar sacred to the Holy Virgin is shown there; a very small one, not worth seeing except as a monument of antiquity, a rebuke to the luxury of our times. There the holy man is said to have spoken his last farewell to the Virgin when death was at hand. On the altar is the point of the sword with which the crown of the good bishop's head was cut off, and his brain evidently smashed to make death come more quickly. Out of love for the martyr we reverently kissed the sacred rust of this sword.

Leaving this place, we went into the crypt. It has its own custodians. First is shown the martyr's skull,[28] pierced through. The top of the cranium is bared for kissing, the rest covered with silver. Along with this is displayed a leaden plate with "Thomas of Acre" [29] carved on it. The hair shirt, girdle, and drawers by which the bishop used to subdue his flesh hang in the gloom there—horrible even to look at, and a reproach to our softness and delicacy.

Menedemus. Perhaps to the monks themselves, too.

Ogygius. I can neither affirm nor deny that, nor is it any of my business.

Menedemus. Very true.

Ogygius. From here we return to the choir. On the north side mysteries are laid open. It is wonderful how many bones were brought forth—skulls, jaws, teeth, hands, fingers, whole

[27] Beneath the steps leading to the choir. Ogygius is being led to the scene of the martyrdom in the northwest transept.

[28] "More probably the new relic of St. Dunstan which had recently been enclosed in a mitred bust of silver, since there is no other record of any part of St. Thomas's head being kept in the crypt" (C. E. Woodruff and W. Danks, *Memorials of the Cathedral and Priory of Christ in Canterbury,* 1912, p. 275).

[29] There was a legend that the saint's mother was a Saracen.

arms, all of which we adored and kissed.[30] This would have gone on forever if my fellow pilgrim, a disagreeable chap, had not cut short the enthusiasm of the guide.

Menedemus. Who was this?

Ogygius. An Englishman named Gratian Pullus,[31] a learned and pious man but less respectful toward this side of religion than I liked.

Menedemus. Some Wycliffite, I suppose.

Ogygius. I don't think so, though he had read his books. Where he got hold of them isn't clear.

Menedemus. Did he offend the guide?

Ogygius. An arm was brought forth, with the bloodstained flesh still on it. He shrank from kissing this, looking rather disgusted. The custodian soon put his things away. Next we viewed the altar table and ornaments; then the objects that were kept under the altar—all of them splendid; you'd say Midas and Croesus were beggars if you saw the quantity of gold and silver.

Menedemus. No kisses here?

Ogygius. No, but a different sort of desire came to my mind.

Menedemus. What was it?

Ogygius. I was sad because I had no such relics at home.

Menedemus. A sacrilegious wish!

Ogygius. Admitted, and I begged the saint's forgiveness before I left the church. After this we were conducted to the sacristy. Good Lord, what an array of silk vestments there, what an abundance of gold candelabra! There, too, we saw St. Thomas' staff. It looked like a cane plated with silver. It was not at all heavy, had no ornamentation, and was no more than waist-high.

---

[30] The relics, we are told, included part of the table at which the Last Supper was eaten and some of the clay out of which God made Adam (Woodruff and Danks, *op. cit.*, pp. 276-277).

[31] "Pullus" ("colt") is undoubtedly John Colet, the Dean of St. Paul's. He was a friend and patron of Erasmus. On the identification see *Erasmi Epistolae*, IV, 517. 327 n.

Menedemus. No cross? [32]

Ogygius. None that I saw. We were shown a pallium, silk to be sure, but coarse, without gold or jewels, and there was a facecloth, soiled by sweat from his neck and preserving obvious spots of blood. These memorials of the plain living of olden times we gladly kissed.

Menedemus. They're not shown to everyone?

Ogygius. Certainly not, my good friend.

Menedemus. How did you manage to make such an impression of devoutness that no secrets were kept from you?

Ogygius. I had some acquaintance with the Reverend Father William Warham,[33] the Archbishop. He gave me a note of recommendation.

Menedemus. I hear from many persons that he is a man of remarkable kindness.

Ogygius. More than that: you would call him kindness itself if you knew him. His learning, integrity, and holiness of life are so great that you would find him lacking in no quality befitting a perfect prelate. Next we were led up above, for behind the high altar you ascend as though into a new church. There, in a small chapel,[34] is shown the entire face [35] of the saint, gilded, and ornamented with many jewels. Here a certain unlooked-for accident almost upset all our good luck.

Menedemus. I'm waiting to hear what misfortune you mean.

Ogygius. My friend Gratian made a *faux pas* here. After a short prayer, he asked the keeper, "I say, good father, is it true, as I've heard, that in his lifetime Thomas was most gen-

[32] I.e., "No cross on the staff?" An archbishop's staff is surmounted by a cross.

[33] He was archbishop from 1504 to 1532. Erasmus, who owed much to his patronage, dedicated his edition of Jerome (1516) to Warham.

[34] The Chapel of the Holy Trinity, at the east end of the church. The shrine was in this chapel.

[35] "This was the mitred bust of St. Thomas which enclosed what at Canterbury was always called Corona—i.e., St. Thomas's crown—but was known to the world as the *Caput sancti Thome* or St. Thomas's head" (Woodruff and Danks, *op. cit.*, p. 279).

erous to the poor?" "Very true," the man replied, and began
to rehearse the saint's many acts of kindness to them. Then
Gratian: "I don't suppose his disposition changed in this
matter, unless perhaps for the better." The custodian agreed.
Gratian again: "Since, then, the saint was so liberal towards
the needy, although he was still poor himself and lacked
money to provide for the necessities of life, don't you think
he'd gladly consent, now that he's so rich and needs nothing,
if some poor wretched woman with hungry children at home,
or daughters in danger of losing their virtue because they have
no money for dowries, or a husband sick in bed and penniless
—if, after begging the saint's forgiveness, she carried off a bit
of all this wealth [36] to rescue her family, as though taking
from one who wanted her to have it, either as a gift or a
loan?" When the keeper in charge of the gilded head made no
reply to this, Gratian, who's impulsive, said, "For my part,
I'm convinced the saint would even rejoice that in death, too,
he could relieve the wants of the poor by his riches." At this
the custodian frowned and pursed his lips, looking at us with
Gorgon eyes, and I don't doubt he would have driven us from
the church with insults and reproaches had he not been aware
that we were recommended by the archbishop. I managed to
placate the fellow by smooth talk, affirming that Gratian
hadn't spoken seriously, but liked to joke; and at the same
time I gave him some coins.

    Menedemus. I quite approve of your sense of duty. But
seriously, I wonder sometimes what possible excuse there
could be for those who spend so much money on building,
decorating, and enriching churches that there's simply no
limit to it. Granted that the sacred vestments and vessels of
the church must have a dignity appropriate to their liturgical
use; and I want the building to have grandeur. But what's
the use of so many baptistries, candelabra, gold statues? What's
the good of the vastly expensive organs, as they call them?

[36] The shrine was later destroyed and the treasures plundered by Henry
VIII. Note Erasmus' prophetic remark in "The Godly Feast," p. 162.

(We're not content with a single pair, either.) What's the good of that costly musical neighing when meanwhile our brothers and sisters, Christ's living temples, waste away from hunger and thirst?

Ogygius. Every decent, sensible man favors moderation in these matters, of course. But since the fault springs from excessive devotion, it merits applause, especially when one thinks of the opposite vice in those who rob churches of their wealth. These gifts are generally given by kings and potentates, and would be worse spent on gambling and war. And removal of anything from there is, in the first place, regarded as sacrilege; next, those who are regular contributors stop their giving; above all, men are incited to robbery. Hence churchmen are custodians of these things rather than owners of them. In short, I'd rather see a church abounding in sacred furnishings than bare and dirty, as some are, and more like stables than churches.

Menedemus. Yet we read that in former times bishops were praised for selling the sacred vessels and using the money to relieve the poor.

Ogygius. They're praised today, too, but only praised. In my judgment, to imitate them is neither allowable nor agreeable.

Menedemus. I'm holding up your story. Let's have the conclusion.

Ogygius. Hear it, then; I'll be brief. While this was going on, the chief official came forward.

Menedemus. Who? The abbot of the place?

Ogygius. He has a miter and abbatical revenue; he lacks only the name of abbot and is called prior,[37] because the archbishop serves instead of an abbot. For in ancient times whoever was archbishop of this diocese was also a monk.

Menedemus. Well, I wouldn't mind being called camel if I had an abbot's income.

Ogygius. He seemed to me a good, sensible man; some-

[37] Thomas Goldston, prior from 1495 to 1517.

thing of a Scotist [38] theologian, too. He opened for us the chest in which the rest of the holy man's body is said to lie.

Menedemus. You saw the bones?

Ogygius. No, that's not allowed, nor would it be possible without the use of ladders. But within the wooden chest is a golden chest; when this is drawn up by ropes, it reveals inestimable treasure.

Menedemus. What do I hear?

Ogygius. The cheapest part was gold. Everything shone and dazzled with rare and surpassingly large jewels, some bigger than a goose egg.[39] Some monks stood about reverently. When the cover was removed, we all adored. The prior pointed out each jewel by touching it with a white rod, adding its French name, its worth, and the name of the donor. The principal ones were gifts from kings.

Menedemus. He must have had a remarkable memory.

Ogygius. Your guess is correct, although practice helps too, for he often does this. From here he leads the way back to the crypt. There the Virgin Mother has a residence, but a somewhat dark one, enclosed by a double row of iron rails.

Menedemus. What's she afraid of?

Ogygius. Only robbers, I suppose, for I've never seen anything more loaded with riches.

Menedemus. You tell me of dark riches.

Ogygius. When the lanterns were brought closer, we saw a more than regal sight.

Menedemus. More wealth than that of St. Mary-by-the-Sea?

Ogygius. It looks like much more. She alone knows her secret wealth. It isn't shown to any but people of the highest importance or to special friends. At last we were led back to the sacristy. There a chest with a black leather cover was

[38] Learned in the philosophy of Duns Scotus, the "subtle doctor." The Scotists were one of the principal schools of philosophers and theologians in the later Middle Ages.

[39] One of these, the "Regale of France," said to have been the gift of King Louis VII, was especially famous.

brought out, placed on the table, and opened. Immediately everyone worshiped on bended knee.

Menedemus. What was inside?

Ogygius. Some linen rags, many of them still showing traces of snivel. With these, they say, the holy man wiped the sweat from his face or neck, the dirt from his nose, or whatever other kinds of filth human bodies have. At this point my friend Gratian again displayed imperfect manners. To him, since he was English, and a well-known person of considerable standing, the prior kindly offered one of the rags as a gift, thinking he was giving him a present that would please him very much. But Gratian was hardly grateful for it. He touched the piece with his fingers, not without a sign of disgust, and put it back scornfully, puckering his lips as though whistling. (This is what he ordinarily did if he came across anything he thought despicable.) Shame and alarm together embarrassed me dreadfully. But the prior, no stupid man, pretended not to notice this incident, and after offering us a glass of wine dismissed us kindly, for we were returning to London.

Menedemus. Why did you have to do that when you were already fairly close to your own shore?

Ogygius. Yes, I was, but I willingly avoided that shore as much as possible. It's more notorious for frauds and robberies than any Malean rocks [40] are for shipwrecks. I'll tell you what I saw on my last crossing. Many of us were ferried in a rowboat from the Calais shore to a larger vessel. Among the passengers was a poor, ragged French youth. He was charged half a drachma; so large a sum do they wring from each passenger for the very short ride. He pleaded poverty. To amuse themselves they search him, and when they pull off his shoes they find ten or twelve drachmas between the soles. These they take, laughing in his face and jeering at the damned Frenchman.

Menedemus. What did the young fellow do?

Ogygius. Mourned his loss. What else could he do?

[40] On the coast of southeastern Peloponnesus.

Menedemus. They had no right to do such things, had they?

Ogygius. Exactly the same right they have to rob passengers' luggage and to snatch purses whenever they get a chance.

Menedemus. It's extraordinary that they should dare to commit such a serious crime in the presence of so many witnesses.

Ogygius. They're so used to doing it that they think it's quite all right. Many persons watched from the larger boat. In the rowboat were some English merchants, who protested in vain. Those fellows boasted about catching the damned Frenchman as if it were a practical joke.

Menedemus. I'd gladly crucify those pirates as a practical joke!

Ogygius. But both shores are full of such men. Guess "what masters might do when knaves dare do such deeds." [41] So from now on I prefer roundabout routes to that short cut. In these respects, just as "the descent to hell is easy" [42] but the return very hard, so entry by this shore is not altogether easy, exit very hard. Some Antwerp sailors were hanging about London; I decided to take my chances with them.

Menedemus. Does that place have such conscientious sailors?

Ogygius. As an ape is always an ape, I confess, so a sailor's always a sailor. But if you compare them with professional thieves, they're angels.

Menedemus. I'll remember that if ever I, too, get the urge to visit that island. But go back to the road I took you away from.

Ogygius. On the way to London, shortly after you leave Canterbury, you find a very deep and narrow road; moreover, it has such steep banks on each side that you can't get out of it. There's no other road you can take, either. On the left side

---

[41] Virgil, *Eclogues,* iii, 16.
[42] Virgil, *Aeneid,* vi, 126-129.

of this road is a little almshouse [43] for some old beggars. As soon as they see a rider coming one of them runs up, sprinkles him with holy water, and presently holds out the upper part of a shoe fastened to a brass rim. In it is a glass that looks like a jewel. People kiss it and make a small contribution.

Menedemus. On that sort of road I'd rather meet a house of old beggars than a gang of able-bodied thieves.

Ogygius. Gratian was riding on my left, closer to the almshouse. He was sprinkled with water, but he managed to put up with that. When the shoe was thrust at him, he asked the man what he meant by this. He said it was St. Thomas' shoe. Gratian turned to me and said heatedly, "What, do these brutes want us to kiss all good men's shoes? Why not, in the same fashion, hold out spittle and other excrements to be kissed?" I felt sorry for the old man and cheered him up with a tip, poor fellow.

Menedemus. In my opinion, Gratian's anger was not entirely unreasonable. If soles of shoes were kept as evidence of a temperate life, I wouldn't object, but I consider it shameless to push soles, shoes, and girdles at one to be kissed. If one kissed them of his own accord, from some overwhelming feeling of piety, I'd think it pardonable.

Ogygius. I won't pretend it wouldn't be better to leave those things undone, but from what can't be amended at a stroke I'm accustomed to take whatever good there is. — Meantime, I was pleasing myself with the reflection that a good man is like a sheep, a bad one like a beast of prey. When an adder's dead, it can't sting, true, but its stench and blood are injurious. A sheep, while alive, nourishes by its milk, provides clothing by its wool, enriches by its offspring; dead, it furnishes useful hide; and all of it can be eaten. So rapacious men, addicted to this world, are troublesome to everybody while alive; when dead, they're a nuisance to the living by reason of the tolling of bells, grandiose funerals, and sometimes by the consecration of their successors—because that means new exactions. Good men, truly, are in every respect

[43] At Harbledown, about two miles from Canterbury.

useful to everyone: as this saint, during his lifetime, encouraged people to holiness by his example, teaching, and exhortations, comforted the forsaken, and raised up the needy. In death his usefulness is almost greater. He built this very wealthy church; he won more power for the clergy throughout England. Lastly, this piece of shoe supports a whole house of poor men.

Menedemus. A noble thought indeed, but since you're of that mind I'm surprised you've never visited St. Patrick's cave,[44] of which marvelous tales are told. To me they're not entirely plausible.

Ogygius. On the contrary, no story about it can be so marvelous that it is not surpassed by the fact itself.

Menedemus. And have you been in it, then?

Ogygius. I sailed in Stygian waters, to be sure; I went down into the jaws of Avernus; I saw what goes on in hell.

Menedemus. You'll do me a favor if you'll be kind enough to tell me about it.

Ogygius. Let this serve as prologue to our conversation; and it's long enough, in my opinion. I'm on my way home to order dinner; I haven't lunched yet.

Menedemus. Why haven't you? Not because of religious observance?

Ogygius. Oh, no, because of a grudge.

Menedemus. A grudge against your belly?

Ogygius. No, against greedy tavern keepers who, though they won't serve a decent meal, don't hesitate to charge their guests outrageous prices. I get even with them in this way: if I expect a good dinner with an acquaintance, or at an innkeeper's who is a little less niggardly, my stomach won't stand much lunch; but if luck has provided the sort of lunch I like, I get a stomach-ache at dinnertime.

Menedemus. Aren't you ashamed to seem so stingy and mean?

---

[44] St. Patrick's Purgatory, a cave in County Donegal, Ulster, which became a place of pilgrimage. According to medieval legend, some pilgrims who went down into the cave witnessed the tortures of hell.

Ogygius. Menedemus, those who take shame into account in such matters, believe me, are bad bookkeepers. I've learned to keep my shame for other purposes.

Menedemus. I long to hear the rest of the tale, so expect me as a guest for dinner. You'll tell it more comfortably there.

Ogygius. Well, thanks very much for inviting yourself, since so many who are pressed to come decline. But my thanks will be doubled if you'll dine at home today, for my time will be taken up with greeting my family. Besides, I have a plan more convenient for us both. Have lunch at *your* home tomorrow for me and my wife. Then I'll talk until dinner—until you admit you're satisfied; and if you like, we won't desert you even at dinner. What are you scratching your head for? You get dinner ready; we'll be sure to come.

Menedemus. I'd prefer stories I wouldn't have to pay for. All right: I'll furnish a bit of lunch, only it will be tasteless unless you season it with good stories.

Ogygius. But look here! Don't you itch to go on these pilgrimages?

Menedemus. Maybe I'll itch after you've finished talking. As matters stand now, I have enough to do by going on my Roman stations.[45]

Ogygius. Roman? You, who've never seen Rome?

Menedemus. I'll tell you. Here's how I wander about at home. I go into the living room and see that my daughter's chastity is safe. Coming out of there into my shop, I watch what my servants, male and female, are doing. Then to the kitchen, to see if any instruction is needed. From here to one place and another, observing what my children and my wife are doing, careful that everything be in order. These are my Roman stations.

Ogygius. But St. James will look after these affairs for you.

Menedemus. Sacred Scripture directs me to take care of them myself. I've never read any commandment to hand them over to saints.

---

[45] Processions to certain churches in Rome on certain days.

✦ VII ✦

THE FUNERAL

First printed 1526. A dramatic and narrative presentation of ideas often expressed by Erasmus in his religious tractates. In his defense of the *Colloquies, De Utilitate Colloquiorum* (1526), he says that in "The Funeral" he reproves the foolish pride of the rich, but declares that he does not defame the religious orders.

Whether George and Cornelius are drawn from life, we do not know. One of the other characters, Vincent the Dominican, does seem recognizable. He is a certain Vincent Theodorici, once of the Sorbonne and from *c.* 1517 of the University of Louvain—a bitter critic of Erasmus and his writings.

MARCOLPHUS, PHAEDRUS

Marcolphus. Where has our Phaedrus been? You're not from the cave of Trophonius,[1] are you?

Phaedrus. Why do you ask that?

Marcolphus. Because you're uncommonly sad, disheveled, dirty, wild-looking: in short, as unlike your name as possible.

Phaedrus. If those who spend their time in coppersmiths' shops are bound to get blackened, why are you surprised if I'm gloomier than usual when I've spent so many days in the company of two sick, dying, and buried men, both of them very dear to me?

Marcolphus. Whose burials are you talking about?

Phaedrus. You know George Balearicus?

Marcolphus. Only by name, not by sight.

---

[1] In Greek legend, Trophonius was swallowed up by the earth. Thereafter he was consulted as an oracle, but those who visited the oracle came back discouraged and melancholy.

The name "Phaedrus" means beaming, cheerful.

Phaedrus. I know you're not acquainted with the other one, Cornelius Montius. We were intimate friends for many years.

Marcolphus. I've never had the experience of being present at a deathbed.

Phaedrus. I have—oftener than I would wish.

Marcolphus. But is death as horrible a thing as it's commonly asserted to be?

Phaedrus. The road leading up to it is harder than death itself. If a man dismisses from his thought the horror and imagination of death, he will have rid himself of a great part of the evil. In brief, whatever torment there is in sickness or death, it is rendered much more endurable if a person surrenders himself wholly to the divine will. For awareness of death, when the soul is already separated from the body, is, I think, either nonexistent or else an extremely low-grade awareness, because before Nature reaches this point it dulls and stuns all areas of sensation.

Marcolphus. We're born without our being aware of it.

Phaedrus. But not without a mother's being aware of it.

Marcolphus. Why don't we die in the same way? Why did God mean death to be such a torture?

Phaedrus. He meant birth to be painful and dangerous for the mother in order that she might love her offspring more dearly. But death he meant to be dreadful for everyone, lest men generally commit suicide. For since, even today, we see so many do violence to themselves, what do you suppose would happen if death weren't horrible? Whenever a servant or even a young son got a thrashing, whenever a wife fell out with her husband, whenever a man lost his money, or something else occurred that upset him, off they'd rush to noose, sword, river, cliff, poison. As matters now stand, the bitterness of death makes life more precious to us, especially since physicians can't cure a man once he's dead. Though all men don't die in the same way, just as they're not all born in the same way. Some find release in a quick death; others sink into a slow death. Persons with sleeping sickness, likewise those stung by an adder, die unconscious, stupefied with sleep. I've noticed this: that no kind of death is so bitter but that it can be endured if one has resolved to die with steadfast mind.

Marcolphus. Which man's death seemed more Christian?

Phaedrus. To me, George's seemed more splendid.

Marcolphus. Does even death have its vainglory?

Phaedrus. Never have I seen two men die so differently. If you have time to listen, I'll describe each one's end. You shall judge which death would be preferable for a Christian.

Marcolphus. Oh, yes, do be good enough to tell me. There's nothing I'd rather hear.

Phaedrus. First hear about George, then. The moment unmistakable signs of death appeared, the company of physicians who had long attended the patient demanded their fees, hiding their feeling of hopelessness about his life.

Marcolphus. How many doctors were there?

Phaedrus. Sometimes ten, sometimes twelve; never fewer than six.

Marcolphus. Enough to kill even a healthy man!

Phaedrus. When they had their money, they warned the relatives confidentially that death was not far off; that they should look to his spiritual welfare, for there was no hope of his physical safety. And the patient was warned courteously by his close friends to entrust his body to God's care, and to concern himself only with what belonged to making a good end. When he heard this, George stared at the physicians in wild surmise, as though indignant at being deserted by them. They retorted that they were physicians, not gods; that what their skill could do had been performed; but that no medicine could prevail against destiny. After this, they went into the next bedroom.

Marcolphus. What? They lingered even after they were paid?

Phaedrus. They had disagreed completely over what sort of disease it was. One said dropsy; another, tympanites; another, an intestinal abscess—each one mentioned a different ailment. And during the whole time they were treating the patient they quarreled violently about the nature of his malady.

Marcolphus. Lucky patient meanwhile!

Phaedrus. To settle their dispute once for all, they requested through his wife that they be permitted later to perform an autopsy on the body—quite a respectable thing, that was, and done customarily as a mark of respect in the case of eminent persons.[2] Furthermore, it would help save many lives, and would increase George's accumulation of merits. Last of all, they promised to buy thirty masses at their own expense for the repose of his soul. This request met with opposition, to be sure, but was finally granted, thanks to their flattery of his wife and relations. Business disposed of, the medical congress adjourned, because it's not right, they say, for those whose job is to save life to look on at death or to attend funerals. Next Bernardine was summoned, a holy man (as you know), warden of the Franciscans; he was to hear confession. Hardly was confession over when the four orders commonly called mendicants caused a disturbance in the house.

Marcolphus. So many vultures at one corpse?

Phaedrus. Then the parish priest was called in, to give the man extreme unction and Holy Communion.

Marcolphus. Piously done.

Phaedrus. Thereupon a bloody battle between the priest and the monks very nearly broke out.[3]

Marcolphus. At the sick man's bedside?

Phaedrus. Yes, and with Christ watching.

Marcolphus. What provoked such unexpected uproar?

Phaedrus. When the priest learned that the patient had confessed to the Franciscan, he declared he would not ad-

---

[2] Cf. Donne, *The Dampe:*

> When I am dead, and Doctors know not why,
>   And my friends curiositie
> Will have me cut up to survey each part . . .

[3] Friction between secular and regular clergy had long been a topic for satire and complaint in literature. Jurisdiction over confession was one cause of the quarrel.

minister the rite of extreme unction, the Eucharist, or burial unless he had heard the patient's confession with his own ears. He was the parish priest; he would have to render an account of his flock to the Lord; this he could not do if he alone were unfamiliar with the secrets of the man's conscience.

Marcolphus. Didn't that seem fair enough?

Phaedrus. Not to them, you may be sure. They all objected vigorously, Bernardine and the Dominican Vincent in particular.

Marcolphus. What was their contribution?

Phaedrus. They fell upon the priest and abused him violently, repeatedly calling him ass and fit for a swineherd. "I," says Vincent, "am a full-fledged Bachelor of Sacred Theology, and soon to be licensed, and even to be distinguished by the title of Doctor. You scarcely read the Gospel, so far are you from being able to probe the secrets of conscience. But if you like to be meddlesome, find out what your wife and bastards are doing at home," and many other remarks of this kind that I'm ashamed to mention.

Marcolphus. What did he do? Did he keep quiet at this?

Phaedrus. Quiet? On the contrary, you'd say a cricket was caught by the wing. "I could make much better bachelors than you are out of beanstalks," says he. "Where did Dominic and Francis, the founders and heads of your orders, learn the Aristotelian philosophy, or the reasonings of Thomas, or the speculations of Scotus? Or where were they granted their bachelor's degrees? You crept into a world still credulous, but you were few, humble, and some of you even learned and holy. You nested in fields and villages. Soon you migrated to some of the wealthiest cities and to the plushiest part of town.[4] You used to work in fields that could not support a shepherd; nowadays you're never anywhere but in rich men's houses. You boast of papal favor, but your privileges are worthless unless a bishop, pastor, or his vicar is inactive. None of you will preach in *my* church so long as I'm in possession as pastor.

[4] This had long been a criticism of the orders, e.g., by Huss in his treatise on simony (1413), vi.

I'm not a bachelor; [5] neither was St. Martin,[6] and yet he served as bishop. If I lack any learning, I won't seek it from you. Or do you believe the world is still so stupid that whenever it sees the garb of Dominic or Francis it thinks their sanctity is present too? Is it any of your business what I do at my own home? What you do in your retreats, how you behave with the nuns, even the public knows. How far from good or decent are the homes of the wealthy that you frequent 'is known to every blear-eyed man and barber.' " [7]

The rest I don't dare repeat, Marcolphus. Altogether he treated those reverend fathers with very little reverence. Nor would there have been any end to this had not George indicated with his hand that he wished to say something. After much effort, the bickering was stilled for a while. Then the sick man said, "Let there be peace among you. I'll confess anew to you, priest. Next, you shall have money paid out to you for the tolling of the bells, funeral dirges, monument, and burial before you leave this house. I'll see to it that you have no reason to complain of me in any respect."

Marcolphus. The priest didn't refuse so fair a bargain as that, did he?

Phaedrus. No. Only he grumbled somewhat about the confession he remitted to the patient. "What need is there," says he, "for tiring both patient and priest by repeating it? If he had confessed to me in time, perhaps his will would have been made more piously. But it's your responsibility now." The sick man's fairness vexed the monks, who were indignant that a share of the booty should fall to the parish priest. But I interceded, and managed to settle the quarrel. The priest anointed the sick man, gave him Communion, and after his money was counted out he left.

Marcolphus. So a calm followed that storm?

Phaedrus. Oh, no, a more severe storm broke out at once.

Marcolphus. What caused it, please?

5 Of Divinity.
6 Of Tours.
7 Horace, *Sat.*, I, vii, 3.

Phaedrus. You'll hear. The four orders of mendicants [8] had poured into the house. They were joined by a fifth, that of the Cross Bearers. Against this order, as a spurious one, these four raised a loud clamor. They asked where the Cross Bearers had ever seen a five-wheeled wagon, or how they had the nerve to want more mendicant orders than there were Evangelists. "In the same fashion," they said, "you might as well bring hither all the beggars from bridges and crossroads."

Marcolphus. What did the Cross Bearers say to this?

Phaedrus. They countered by asking how the wagon of the Church had run when no order of mendicants existed; then, how it ran when there was one, and later three. "For the number of the Evangelists," they said, "has no more connection with our orders than with dice, which show four corners on every side. Who elected the Augustinians to the order of mendicants? Or who the Carmelites? When did Augustine beg, or when Elijah?" [9] (For these men they make the founders of their orders.) This and much else they thundered boldly indeed, but, unable by themselves to withstand the onslaught of the four orders, they retreated, only with dire threats.

Marcolphus. You enjoyed calm weather after that, surely?

Phaedrus. Not at all. That alliance against the fifth order turned into a gladiatorial combat. Franciscan and Dominican contended that neither Augustinians nor Carmelites were genuine mendicants, but bastard and spurious. This dispute raged so furiously that I was quite afraid it would come to blows.

Marcolphus. Did the patient put up with this?

Phaedrus. It didn't take place at the bedside, but in the hall next to the chamber. Nevertheless every word reached

[8] Dominicans, Franciscans, Augustinians, and Carmelites. Rivalry among the orders was another favorite topic of their critics. The Cross Bearers are the Crutched or Crossed Friars, who wore a cross of red cloth on their habit.

[9] Because they claimed descent from Elijah and Elisha, the Carmelites considered themselves the most ancient of the religious orders.

him, since they weren't whispering but playing the piece *fortissimo*. Even apart from this, as you know, invalids have rather sensitive hearing.

Marcolphus. How did the war end?

Phaedrus. Through his wife, the patient asked them to quiet down a little and he would compose the quarrel. So he requested the Augustinians and Carmelites to leave at once; they would lose nothing by doing so. "For," said he, "as much food will be sent to them at their house as is given to those remaining here." He directed all the orders, even the fifth one, to attend his funeral, and a sum of money to be divided equally among them. But to prevent disorder he forbade them to come to the wake.

Marcolphus. Evidently he was a good manager, who even when dying knew how to still the waves.

Phaedrus. Tush! He'd been a general in the army for many years. Disturbances of this kind in the ranks are an everyday occurrence there.

Marcolphus. Was he rich?

Phaedrus. Very.

Marcolphus. But with ill-gotten gains, as it happens, from robberies, sacrileges, and extortions.

Phaedrus. Of course; that's the custom for generals. I wouldn't swear he was different from the rest in his ways. If I knew the man well, however, he grew rich by his wits rather than by violence.

Marcolphus. How so?

Phaedrus. He was clever at accounting.

Marcolphus. What of it?

Phaedrus. What of it? He reported 30,000 troops to his commander when there were scarcely 7,000. Next, to many soldiers he paid nothing at all.

Marcolphus. A rich accounting indeed!

Phaedrus. Then, he waged war scientifically. He used to contract for monthly payments at the same time by villages and towns of both friend and foe: from the enemy, so fighting wouldn't break out; from friends, for allowing them to trade with the enemy.

Marcolphus. I'm familiar with the common practice of military men. But finish your story.

Phaedrus. So Bernardine and Vincent, with some fellow-members of their orders, remained with the sick man. Provisions were sent to the others.

Marcolphus. Did those who held the fort get along satisfactorily?

Phaedrus. Not in every respect. They were muttering something or other about privileges granted by papal briefs, but they pretended not to, for fear their business wouldn't get finished. At this time the last will and testament was produced, and covenants were made in the presence of witnesses concerning those matters they had already settled among themselves.

Marcolphus. I can't wait to hear these.

Phaedrus. I'll summarize them, because it's a long story. He was survived by a wife of 38, a good sensible woman; two sons, one 19, the other 15; as many daughters, but both young and unmarried. The will provided that since the wife could not be induced to become a nun she should put on a Beguine's cloak—an order midway between nuns and laywomen [10]—and the elder son, since he flatly refused to become a monk—

Marcolphus. You don't catch an old fox with a noose!

Phaedrus. —was to hurry to Rome without delay after his father's funeral. There, after being made priest by a papal dispensation before reaching legal age, he should say mass for his father's soul every day for a whole year in the Vatican church, and every Friday crawl on his knees up the sacred steps [11] in the Lateran church.

---

[10] They lived according to religious discipline while in the community, but did not take perpetual vows, and could leave the community whenever they wished.

[11] The Scala Sancta, marble steps traditionally believed to have been brought by St. Helena from Jerusalem, where they belonged to Pilate's palace and thus were trodden by Christ.

Marcolphus. Was he glad to undertake this?

Phaedrus. To be blunt, he was as glad as asses are to bear heavy burdens. The younger son was promised to St. Francis, the older daughter to St. Clare,[12] the younger daughter to St. Catherine of Siena.[13] Only this last promise could be kept. George's intention was to have God further in his debt by putting his five survivors into five mendicant orders, and he tried very hard to do so, but his wife's age and that of his elder son would yield neither to threats nor to flattery.

Marcolphus. A way of disinheriting them.

Phaedrus. The entire estate was so divided that after money for funeral expenses was set aside, one share was allotted to the wife: half of this for her support, half to the house she would join. If she changed her mind and backed out of the agreement, all the money was to pass to that congregation. Another share would fall to the son. He, however, would have passage money paid to him at once, and enough to buy the dispensation and take care of a year's living expenses in Rome. If he changed his mind and refused to take priestly orders, his share would be divided between the Franciscans and Dominicans. And I fear that may happen, so greatly did the boy seem to detest a priestly career. Two shares would go to the monastery receiving the younger son; two likewise to the nunneries receiving the daughters, but on condition that if these children balked at entering the religious life, the monastery and nunneries could still keep all the money. Furthermore, one share would go presently to Bernardine; the same amount to Vincent; half a share to the Carthusians, for the community of all good works done by the entire order. The one-and-a-half shares remaining were to be distributed to undisclosed beggars approved by Bernardine and Vincent.

---

12 I.e., to the Poor Clares, the Second Order of St. Francis, named after St. Clare of Assisi.

13 I.e., to the Third Order of St. Dominic, of which St. Catherine was a member.

Marcolphus. You should have said, lawyer-fashion, "those beggars male and female."

Phaedrus. So when the will had been read, the covenants were made in the following terms: "Do you, George Balearicus, being alive and of sound mind, approve this testament which you have made of recent date and in accordance with your wishes?" "I do." "And is this your final and irrevocable will?" "It is." "And do you appoint me and the said Vincent, Bachelor, executors of your last will?" "I do." He was ordered to sign it again.

Marcolphus. How could a dying man do that?

Phaedrus. Bernardine guided the invalid's hand.

Marcolphus. What did he write down?

Phaedrus. "May he who attempts henceforth to change any of this incur the wrath of St. Francis and St. Dominic."

Marcolphus. But weren't they afraid of a suit on grounds of "inofficious testament"? [14]

Phaedrus. That kind of suit doesn't apply to property promised to God, nor does anyone readily sue God at law. When these matters were finished, the wife and children gave their right hand to the sick man and swore they would keep the obligations laid upon them.[15] After that, the funeral procession came up for discussion [16]—but not without argument. Finally they agreed that from each of the five orders nine members should attend, in honor of the five books of Moses and the nine choirs of angels: each order to carry its own cross before it and sing funeral dirges. With these and the relatives should march thirty torchbearers dressed in black (thirty being the number of coins for which the Lord was sold), and—to lend distinction—twelve mourners (the number sacred to the band of Apostles, that is) should accompany

[14] In Roman and civil law, a testament invalid because it deprived an heir of the portion of the estate to which he was entitled.

[15] In a letter written three years prior to the publication of this colloquy, Erasmus had mentioned *uxor morosa* and *liberi inobedientes* as common afflictions at deathbeds (*Erasmi Epistolae*, V, 241. 126-128).

[16] In *The Praise of Folly* (cf. H. H. Hudson's translation, 1941, p. 59), exactness in prescribing arrangements for one's funeral is ridiculed.

them. The bier should be followed by George's horse, draped in black, with his head tied down to his knees to suggest that he was looking along the ground for his master. Coverlets hanging from here and there on the bier were to display George's decorations. Likewise each torch and mourning garb should have decorations. Now the body itself was to rest at the right of the high altar in a marble tomb, four feet high. On top of the tomb was to be George's effigy carved in Parian marble, in full armor from head to foot. His helmet was to have his crest (a pelican's neck), and his left arm a shield bearing as insignia three boars' heads of gold in a field of silver. Nor was his sword with the golden hilt to be missing from his side, nor his gold baldric decorated with jeweled studs, nor his gold spurs from his feet; for he was a gilded knight. At his feet he was to have a leopard. The borders of the tomb were to have an inscription worthy of such a man. He wanted his heart to be buried separately in the chapel of St. Francis. His entrails he bequeathed to the parish priest for honorable burial in a chapel sacred to the Virgin Mother.

Marcolphus. A splendid funeral, no doubt, but too costly. At Venice any cobbler would be accorded a more splendid one for a minimum of expense. His guild gives a fine bier; and sometimes six hundred monks, dressed in tunics or cloaks, accompany a single body.

Phaedrus. I too have seen and laughed at this inappropriate ostentation of the poor.[17] Fullers and tanners march in front, cobblers in the rear, monks in the middle; you'd say they were chimeras. Nor would you have seen any difference here. George stipulated also that Franciscan and Dominican were to settle by lot which of them should have first place in the procession; then the rest, too, were to draw lots, to prevent any disorder on this account. The parish priest and his clerks were to have last place, i.e., march first, for the monks would consent to no other arrangement.

Marcolphus. He was skilled in drawing up not only battle lines but parades as well.

17 Erasmus lived for a year in Venice (1507-1508).

Phaedrus. It was stipulated, too, that the funeral service, conducted by the parish priest, should be accompanied by music, softly played, in George's honor. During the negotiations over these and other matters, the sick man shuddered and gave unmistakable signs of having reached his last moment. The final act of the play was therefore prepared.

Marcolphus. We're not at the end yet?

Phaedrus. A papal brief [18] was read, promising forgiveness of all sins and banishing fear of purgatory entirely. In addition, all his goods were accounted rightful.

Marcolphus. The "goods" he got by robbery?

Phaedrus. By the law of war and military custom, surely. But Philip the lawyer, his brother-in-law, chanced to be present. He noticed in the papal brief a passage that was out of order, and raised the question of fraud.

Marcolphus. Not at that time! Even if there was some mistake, it should have been suppressed, and the sick man would have been none the worse.

Phaedrus. I agree. And the sick man was so upset by this news that he was almost in despair. At this juncture Vincent proved himself a man. He told George not to worry, that he himself had authority to correct and supplement any error or omission in the brief. "If," says he, "the brief fails you, I hereby substitute my own soul for yours, so that yours goes to heaven and mine is abandoned to hell."

Marcolphus. Does God accept such exchanges of souls? And if so, did such a pledge seem sufficient security for George? What if Vincent's soul was due for hell without any exchange?

Phaedrus. I'm telling you what happened. Unquestionably Vincent did succeed in causing the sick man to take heart. Next, articles were recited by which George was promised partnership in the community of all works done by the four orders, and by the fifth, the Cross Bearers.

Marcolphus. I'd be afraid of sinking down to hell if I had to carry so great a load.

[18] *Diploma.* A plenary indulgence seems to be meant.

Phaedrus. I mean *good* works. They no more burden the soul in its upward flight than wings do a bird.

Marcolphus. Then to whom do they bequeath their evil works?

Phaedrus. To German mercenaries.[19]

Marcolphus. By what warrant?

Phaedrus. By gospel warrant: "Whosoever hath, to him shall be given." [20] At the same time a number—an enormous number—of masses and psalms were recited; these were to accompany the soul of the deceased. Then confession was repeated and the blessing given.

Marcolphus. And so he breathed his last?

Phaedrus. Not yet. A rush mat was spread on the floor in such a manner that at one end it looked like a pillow.

Marcolphus. Now what's going to happen?

Phaedrus. They scattered a few ashes on it, and there they laid the sick man. A Franciscan tunic was spread over him, but only after being blessed by short prayers and holy water. A cowl was placed at his head (for at that time it could not be put on), and along with that his brief and the covenants.[21]

Marcolphus. A new kind of death!

Phaedrus. But they swear the devil has no jurisdiction over those who die thus. So, they say, St. Martin and St. Francis, among others, died.

Marcolphus. But *their* lives corresponded to this kind of death. What happened after that, please?

Phaedrus. A crucifix and a taper were held out to the sick man. To the crucifix extended to him he said, "In war I was accustomed to rely on my shield; now will I face my foe with this shield." And after he kissed it, he turned on his left side. To the taper he said, "I used to excel with my spear in

19 As his writings on war and government show, Erasmus detested the mercenaries (Swiss and Germans, mostly) of his day.

20 Matthew 13:12.

21 Erasmus satirizes this custom in another colloquy, "The Seraphic Funeral."

war; now will I brandish this spear against the enemy of souls."

Marcolphus. Spoken like a soldier!

Phaedrus. These were his last words, for presently death stopped his tongue and at the same moment he began to expire. Bernardine on his right, Vincent on his left, hung over the dying man, both in fine voice. One displayed an image of St. Francis, the other that of Dominic. Others, scattered through the bedroom, murmured some psalms in a doleful tone. Bernardine assailed his right ear with great clamors, Vincent his left.

Marcolphus. What were they screaming?

Phaedrus. Bernardine something like this: "George Balearicus, if now you approve what's been done between us, turn your head to the right." He did so. Vincent, on the other side: "Be not afraid, George, you have Francis and Dominic as your champions. Rest easy: think how many merits you have, what a papal brief; finally, remember my soul is pledged for yours if there is any danger. If you understand and approve this, nod your head to the left." He nodded. Again, with like clamor: "If you understand this," he says, "press my hand." Then George pressed his hand. So what with nodding to this side and that, and pressing of hands, nearly three hours were spent. Just as George began to gape, Bernardine, standing up straight, pronounced the absolution, but George was dead before he could finish it. This occurred at midnight. In the morning the autopsy was performed.

Marcolphus. What disease did they find in his body?

Phaedrus. I'm glad you brought that up, because it had slipped my mind. A piece of lead was lodged in his diaphragm.

Marcolphus. Where did that come from?

Phaedrus. His wife told us he had once been struck there by a bullet. Hence the physicians conjectured that a fragment of the melted lead was left in his body. Soon the mangled body was clothed somehow or other in a Franciscan cloak. After lunch burial was made, with that procession which had been arranged.

Marcolphus. I've never heard of a more troublesome death nor of a more pretentious funeral. But you wouldn't want this story to get out, I suppose.

Phaedrus. Why not?

Marcolphus. To avoid stirring up a hornets' nest.

Phaedrus. No danger. For if what I tell is righteous, it concerns these very men that the public should know it; if less than righteous, as many of them as are good will thank me for bringing it to light. Some, made ashamed of themselves, may stop doing things like this. Next, uneducated persons may take warning against making a similar mistake. For the sincere and genuinely religious men among them have often complained to me that because of the superstition or dishonesty of a few, an entire order is rendered odious among respectable people.

Marcolphus. Well said, and boldly. But now I'm impatient to hear how Cornelius died.

Phaedrus. As he lived without being a nuisance to anyone, so he died. He had an annual fever that recurred regularly. And then, either because of his old age—for he was past sixty—or for some other reason, it oppressed him more than usual, and he himself seemed to sense that his last day was close at hand. So, four days before his death, i.e., on Sunday, he went to church, confessed to his parish priest, heard sermon and mass, devoutly took Communion, and returned home.

Marcolphus. He didn't use physicians?

Phaedrus. He consulted only one, but one who was fully as good a man as he was a physician: James Castrutius by name.

Marcolphus. I know him. No man is truer.

Phaedrus. He promised to do whatever he could for his friend, but said he thought there was more help in God than in doctors. Cornelius received this reply as cheerfully as if he had been given absolute assurance of life. And so, even though he had always been as liberal towards the poor as his means permitted, he then distributed among the destitute whatever he could spare from the needs of his wife and children; not to pushing and sometimes obtrusive beggars, but to worthy ones who struggled against their poverty by working as hard as they could. I implored him to go to bed and summon the priest rather than exhaust his weak body. He replied that he had always tried to help his friends, if possible, rather than be under obligation to them; nor did he want to be any different at death. He didn't even take to his bed except for the last day and part of the night on which he left this earth. Meanwhile he used a cane because of his physical weakness, or sat in a big chair. Occasionally he lay down on a little bed, but with his clothes on and his head up. At this time he either gave instructions for relieving the poor, particularly those who were acquaintances or neighbors, or he read from the Bible passages exhorting man to trust God, and setting forth God's love for us. If weakness prevented him from doing even this for himself, he listened while a friend read. Often, with wonderful feeling, he urged his family to mutual love and harmony and to zeal for true righteousness, and comforted them very affectionately, grieved as they were about his dying. From time to time he reminded his family not to leave any of his debts unpaid.

Marcolphus. Hadn't he made a will?

Phaedrus. He had attended to that long before, when he was well and strong. For he held that those made by the dying weren't wills but rather ravings.

Marcolphus. Didn't he bequeath anything to monasteries or to the poor?

Phaedrus. Not a farthing. "I have shared my modest fortune as I could afford," he said. "Now, as I am handing over possession of it to others, so I hand over the spending of it. And I am confident that my family will spend it better than I myself have done."

Marcolphus. Didn't he send for holy men, as George did?

Phaedrus. Not even one. Except his family and two close friends, nobody was present.

Marcolphus. I wonder why he felt like that.

Phaedrus. He insisted he didn't want to be troublesome

to more people when dying than he had been when he was born.

Marcolphus. I'm awaiting the end of this story.

Phaedrus. You'll soon hear it. Thursday came. Feeling extremely weak, he did not leave his couch. The parish priest was called, gave him extreme unction, and again administered Communion, but without confession, for Cornelius said he had no lingering anxieties on his mind. At that point the priest began to discuss the funeral—what sort of procession, and where he was to be buried. "Bury me as you would the humblest Christian," he said. "It makes no difference to me where you lay this poor body; it will be found on the Last Day just the same, wherever you've put it. The funeral procession I care nothing about." Presently the subjects of tolling the bells, thirty-day and anniversary masses, a papal brief, and purchase of a community of merits came up. Then he said, "Pastor, I'll be none the worse off if no bell tolls; or if you deem me worthy of one burial service, that will be more than enough. Or if there is anything else that because of the Church's public custom can scarcely be omitted without scandal to the weak, I leave that to your judgment. I do not desire to buy up someone's prayers or deprive anyone of his merits. There is sufficient abundance of merits in Christ, and I have faith that the prayers and merits of the whole Church will benefit me, if only I am a true member of it. In two 'briefs' I rest my entire hope. One is the fact that the Lord Jesus, the chief shepherd, took away my sins, nailing them to the Cross. The other, that which he signed and sealed with his own sacred blood, by which he assured us of eternal salvation if we place our whole trust in him. For far be it from me that, equipped with merits and briefs, I should summon my Lord to court with his servant, certain as I am that in his sight shall no man living be justified! [22] For my part, I appeal from his justice to his mercy, since it is boundless and inexpressible." Whereupon the priest departed. Eager and joyous, as though with strong hope of salvation, Cornelius ordered

22 Psalms 143:2.

certain biblical passages confirming the hope of resurrection and rewards of immortality to be read to him: as that in Isaiah [23] on the postponement of Hezekiah's death, along with his hymn; then the fifteenth chapter of Paul's first letter to the Corinthians; the story of Lazarus' death from John; [24] but above all, the narrative of Christ's passion from the Gospels. How eagerly he concentrated on every one of these, sighing at some, giving thanks with folded hands at others, at some rejoicing and exulting, at others uttering brief prayers! After lunch, when he had taken a short nap, he had the twelfth chapter of John read, to the very end. When this was done, you would have said the man was completely transformed and breathed upon by a new spirit.

Day was already turning to evening. He called for his wife and children; then, straightening up as much as his weakness permitted, he spoke to his family thus: "My dearest wife, those whom earlier God had joined together, now likewise he puts asunder; but in body only, and that for a little while. The care, love, and devotion you have been accustomed to share with me and our sweetest children, transfer wholly to them. Do not suppose you can deserve better by any means, either of God or of me, than by so nurturing, cherishing, and instructing those whom God gave us as the fruits of our marriage, that they may be accounted worthy of Christ. Double your devotion towards them, therefore, and consider my share made over to you. If you do that—as I am confident you will—there will be no reason they should seem orphans. But if you remarry"—at this word his wife broke into tears and began to swear she would never think of marrying again. Then Cornelius: "My dearest sister in Christ, if the Lord Jesus shall think best to grant you that resolution and strength of spirit, do not fail the heavenly gift, for this will be more comfortable for you and the children alike. But if weakness of the flesh shall call otherwise, know that my death releases you from the marriage bond, but not from the obligation you

[23] Isaiah 38; II Kings 20:1-11.
[24] John 11:1-45.

have in my name, and in your own, of caring for our children. As for marrying, use the liberty the Lord has given you. This only do I ask, and warn you of: that you choose a husband of such moral character, and bear yourself towards him in such a way, that, guided by his own kindness and prompted by your gentleness, he may love his stepchildren. Be cautious, therefore, about binding yourself by any vow. Keep yourself free for God and for our children. So train them to every form of godliness that you may dissuade them from committing themselves to any career before age and experience demonstrate what mode of life they are suited for." Turning then to his children, he exhorted them to the pursuit of righteousness, to obedience to their mother, to mutual love and concord among themselves. Having spoken these words, he kissed his wife, made the sign of the Cross, and invoked the favor and mercy of Christ upon his children. After that, looking upon all who were present, he said, "By dawn tomorrow the Lord who rose from the dead at daybreak will of His mercy vouchsafe to call this poor soul from the tomb of this poor body, and from the shades of this mortality into His heavenly light. I do not want to tire tender youth with vain watching. Let the others, too, take turns sleeping. I need only one watcher, to read the sacred page."

When the night had passed—it was about four o'clock—and all were come, he ordered read the entire psalm [25] spoken by the Lord when praying on the Cross. After it was ended, he bade them bring a taper and a crucifix. And taking the taper he said, "The Lord is my light and my salvation: whom shall I fear?" [26] Kissing the crucifix, he said, "The Lord is the strength of my life: of whom shall I be afraid?" Presently he folded his hands on his breast, in the manner of one praying, and with his eyes turned to heaven said, "Lord Jesus, receive my spirit." And straightway he closed his eyes as though he were going to sleep, and at the same time expired with a slight gasp. You would have said he had fallen asleep, not died.

25 Psalms 22.
26 Psalms 27:1.

Marcolphus. I never heard of a death less troublesome.

Phaedrus. He was like that all his life. Each of these men was my friend. Perhaps I'm not a fair judge of which one died in a manner more becoming a Christian. You, being unprejudiced, will decide that better.

Marcolphus. I'll do so, but at my leisure.

❧ VIII ☙

CHARON

First printed 1529. A good example of Erasmian satire of war and warmongers. In tone and setting, "Charon" recalls similar pieces by Lucian, one of Erasmus' favorite writers.

In Greek mythology Charon was the ferryman who took the souls of the dead over the river Styx. Alastor was an avenging spirit.

CHARON, THE SPIRIT ALASTOR

Charon. Why the hustle and bustle, Alastor?

Alastor. Well met, Charon! I was speeding to you.

Charon. What's new?

Alastor. I bring news that will delight you and Proserpina.[1]

Charon. Out with it, then. Unload it.

Alastor. The Furies have done their work with as much zeal as success. Not a corner of the earth have they left unravaged by their hellish dissensions—wars, robberies, plagues: so much so that now, with their snakes let loose, they're completely bald.[2] Drained of poisons, they roam about, looking for whatever vipers and asps they can find, since they're as smooth-headed as an egg—not a hair on their crowns, nor a drop of good poison in their breasts. So get your boat and oars ready, for there'll soon be such a crowd of shades coming that I fear you can't ferry them all.

Charon. No news to me.

Alastor. Where did you learn it?

Charon. Ossa [3] brought it more than two days ago.

1 Queen of the underworld.

2 The Furies had poisonous snakes for hair. These they sent to torment the consciences of the wicked.

3 In Homer, the goddess Rumor.

Alastor. Can't get ahead of that goddess! But why are you loitering here without your boat, then?

Charon. Business trip: I came here to get a good, strong trireme ready. My galley's so rotten with age and so patched up that it won't do for this job, if what Ossa told me is true. Though what need was there of Ossa? The plain fact of the matter demands it: I've had a shipwreck.

Alastor. You *are* dripping wet, undoubtedly. I thought you were coming back from a bath.

Charon. Oh, no, I've been swimming out of the Stygian swamp.

Alastor. Where have you left the shades?

Charon. Swimming with the frogs.

Alastor. But what did Ossa report?

Charon. That the three rulers of the world, in deadly hatred, clash to their mutual destruction.[4] No part of Christendom is safe from the ravages of war, for those three have dragged all the rest into alliance. They're all in such a mood that none of them is willing to yield to another. Neither Dane nor Pole nor Scot nor Turk,[5] in fact, is at peace; catastrophes are building up; the plague rages everywhere, in Spain, Britain, Italy, France. In addition, there's a new

---

[4] The passage refers to the recent course of the Italian wars. The three rulers are Charles V, Holy Roman Emperor, Francis I, king of France, and Henry VIII, king of England. Francis had been captured at the battle of Pavia (1525). When the Treaty of Madrid was signed and Francis released by the Spanish, he immediately joined with Milan, Venice, Florence, and the papacy in a league against Charles. England supported the league unofficially. In the Italian campaigns that followed, the fighting mostly favored the Imperial forces. It culminated in the Sack of Rome by undisciplined Imperial forces in May, 1527, the most spectacular disaster suffered by the papacy in centuries. Henry VIII had now joined Francis, and gave the war his active assistance. A new Italian campaign opened, but after six months the pope, warned by Imperial successes, began efforts to make a peace. Charles rejected the terms, and the war went on until August, 1529. By that time the Empire had won control of Italy.

[5] The Turks had crushed the Hungarian army in the battle of Mohacs, August, 1526.

epidemic,[6] born of difference of opinion. It has so corrupted everybody's mind that sincere friendship exists nowhere, but brother distrusts brother, and husband and wife disagree. I have hopes of a splendid slaughter in the near future, too, if the war of tongues and pens comes to actual blows.

Alastor. Ossa reported all this quite correctly, for I've seen more than this with my own eyes; I, the constant attendant and assistant of the Furies, who have never shown themselves more deserving of their name.

Charon. But there's danger that some devil may turn up and preach peace all of a sudden—and mortal minds are fickle. I hear there's a certain Polygraphus [7] up there who's incessantly attacking war with his pen and urging men to peace.

Alastor. He's sung to deaf ears this long while. He once wrote a "Complaint of Peace O'erthrown"; now he's written the epitaph of peace dead and buried. On the other hand, there are some who are as helpful to our cause as the Furies themselves.

Charon. Who are those?

Alastor. Certain creatures in black and white cloaks and ash gray tunics, adorned with plumage of various kinds.[8] They never leave the courts of princes. They instill into their ears a love of war; they incite rulers and populace alike; they proclaim in their evangelical sermons that war is just, holy, and right. And—to make you marvel more at the audacity of the fellows—they proclaim the very same thing on both sides. To the French they preach that God is on the French side: he who has God to protect him cannot be conquered! To the English and Spanish they declare this war is not the emperor's but God's: only let them show themselves valiant men and victory is certain! But if anyone *does* get killed, he doesn't perish utterly but flies straight up to heaven, armed just as he was.

Charon. And people believe these men?

6 Lutheranism.

7 Erasmus.

8 The friars.

Alastor. What can a pretense of religion not achieve?
Youth, inexperience, thirst for glory, anger, and natural
human inclination swallow this whole. People are easily im-
posed upon. And it's not hard to upset a cart that's ready to
collapse of its own accord.

Charon. I'll be glad to reward these creatures!

Alastor. Give them a fine dinner. They like nothing
better.

Charon. A dinner of mallows, lupines, and leeks. That's
the only fare we have, as you know.

Alastor. Oh, no, it must be partridges, capons, and
pheasants if you wish to be an acceptable host.

Charon. But what makes them such warmongers? Or what
advantage are they afraid of losing?

Alastor. They make more profit from the dying than from
the living. There are wills, masses for kinsmen, bulls, and
many other sources of revenue not to be despised. In short,
they prefer to buzz in camp rather than in their own hives.
War spawns many bishops who in peacetime weren't worth a
penny.

Charon. They're smart.

Alastor. But why do you need a trireme?

Charon. I don't, if I want to be shipwrecked in the middle
of the swamp again.

Alastor. On account of the crowd?

Charon. Of course.

Alastor. But you haul shades, not bodies. Just how light
are shades?

Charon. They may be water skippers, but enough water
skippers could sink a boat. Then, you know, the boat is un-
substantial, too.

Alastor. But sometimes, I remember, when there was a
crowd so large the boat couldn't hold them all, I saw three
thousand shades hanging from your rudder, and you didn't
feel any weight.

Charon. I grant there are such souls, which departed
little by little from bodies worn away by consumption or

hectic fever. But those plucked on the sudden from heavy bodies bring a good deal of bodily substance along with them. Apoplexy, quinsy, plague, but especially war, send this kind.

Alastor. Frenchmen or Spaniards don't weigh much, I suppose.

Charon. Much less than others, though even their souls are not exactly featherweight. But from well-fed Britons and Germans such shades come at times that lately I've hardly dared to ferry even ten, and unless I'd thrown them overboard I'd have gone down along with boat, rowers, and passage money.

Alastor. A terrible risk!

Charon. Meanwhile what do you think is going to happen when heavy lords, Thrasos, and swashbucklers come along?

Alastor. None of those who die in a just war [9] come to you, I believe. For these, they say, fly straight to heaven.

Charon. Where they may fly to, I don't know. I do know one thing: that whenever a war's on, so many come to me wounded and cut up that I'd be surprised if any had been left on earth. They come loaded not only with debauchery and gluttony but even with bulls, benefices, and many other things.

Alastor. But they don't bring these along with them. The souls come to you naked.

Charon. True, but newcomers bring along dreams of such things.

Alastor. So dreams are heavy?

Charon. They weigh down my boat. Weigh down, did I say? They've already sunk it! Finally, do you imagine so many obols weigh nothing?

Alastor. Well, I suppose they *are* heavy if they're copper ones.

Charon. So I've decided to look out for a vessel strong enough for the load.

Alastor. Lucky you!

[9] Erasmus believed that if there is such a thing as a just war, it is one fought in self-defense after one's country has been invaded. But he thought "just" wars seldom occurred.

Charon. How so?

Alastor. Because you'll soon grow rich.

Charon. From a lot of shades?

Alastor. Of course.

Charon. If only they'd bring their riches with them! As it is, those in the boat who lament the kingdoms, prelacies, abbacies, and countless talents of gold they left up there bring me nothing but an obol. And so everything I've scraped together in three thousand years has to be laid out for one trireme.

Alastor. If you want to make money, you have to spend money.

Charon. Yet mortals, as I hear, do business better: with Mercury's help they grow rich within three years.

Alastor. But sometimes those same mortals go broke. Your profit is less, but it's more certain.

Charon. How certain I can't tell. If some god should turn up now and settle the affairs of princes, my whole fortune would be lost.

Alastor. Don't give the matter a thought; just leave it to me. You've no reason to fear a peace within ten whole years.[10] Only the Roman pontiff is zealous in urging peace, but his efforts are wasted. Cities, too, weary of their troubles, complain bitterly. People—I don't know who they are—mutter that it's outrageous for human affairs to be turned topsy-turvy on account of the personal grudges or ambitions of two or three men. But the Furies, believe me, will defeat counsel, no matter how good it is. —Yet what need was there for you to ask this favor of those above? Haven't we workmen of our own? We have Vulcan, surely.

Charon. Fine—if I wanted a bronze ship.

Alastor. Labor's cheap.

Charon. Yes, but we're short of timber.

Alastor. What, aren't there any forests here?

---

[10] In fact, peace was made a few months after this colloquy appeared. The Empire was victorious in Italy, and by the Treaty of Cambrai (August, 1529) France renounced its claim to Italian territory.

Charon. Even the groves in the Elysian fields have been used up.

Alastor. What for?

Charon. For burning shades of heretics. So that we've been forced of late to mine coal from the depths of the earth.

Alastor. What, can't those shades be punished at less expense?

Charon. This was the decision of Rhadamanthus.[11]

Alastor. When you've bought your trireme, where will you get rowers?

Charon. My job is to hold the tiller; the shades must row if they want passage.

Alastor. But some haven't learned how to handle an oar.

Charon. No distinction of persons with me: monarchs row and cardinals row, each in their turn, no less than common folk, whether they've learned or not.

Alastor. Good luck in getting a trireme at a bargain! I won't hold you up any longer. I'll take the good news to Orcus.[12] But say, Charon—

Charon. What?

Alastor. Hurry back, so the crowd won't quickly overwhelm you.

Charon. Oh, you'll meet over two hundred thousand on the bank already, besides those swimming in the swamp. But I'll hurry as much as I can. Tell 'em I'll be there right away.

[11] One of the judges of the dead.
[12] God of the underworld.

CYCLOPS, OR THE GOSPEL BEARER

First printed 1529. The speakers' names are those of
Erasmus' servants at the time. Nicholas Cannius, of Amster-
dam, was a member of his household from May, 1527, until
1530, when he returned to Holland. Later he became a
priest. Felix Rex, of Ghent, seems to have had the nickname
Polyphemus ("many-voiced") because of his knowledge of
languages, but here of course it serves to identify him with
Polyphemus the Cyclops, in the *Odyssey*. He was in Erasmus'
service, mostly as a letter-carrier, for about a year, 1528-
1529. In 1534 he became a librarian to Duke Albert of
Prussia. He was evidently a man of parts, but reckless,
quarrelsome, and given to drink. Erasmus was glad to see
the last of him.

Both Cannius and Polyphemus wanted to appear in the
Colloquies, Erasmus tells us (*Erasmi Epistolae,* VIII, 135.
14-15, 18). Polyphemus, who talked of enlisting against the
Turks when he left Erasmus' service, is presented in the
dialogue as a typical soldier, as soldiers are commonly por-
trayed in Erasmus' writings.

CANNIUS, POLYPHEMUS

Cannius. What's Polyphemus hunting here?

Polyphemus. What could I be hunting without dogs or
spear? Is that your question?

Cannius. Some wood nymph, perhaps.

Polyphemus. A good guess. Look, here's my hunting net.

Cannius. What a sight! Bacchus in a lion's skin [1]—Polyphemus with a book—a cat in a saffron gown! [2]

---

[1] Bacchus was represented as somewhat effeminate, but once when captured by pirates and taken aboard ship he changed into a lion; the
sailors, terrified, jumped overboard. The story is told in Homer's Seventh
Hymn. The probability that Erasmus had this in mind is strengthened by
Cannius' reference to a pirate a few moments later.

[2] A Greek proverb about something outlandish or fantastically inappropriate.

Polyphemus. I've painted this little book not only in saffron but bright red and blue, too.

Cannius. I'm not talking about saffron; I said something in Greek. Seems to be a soldierly book, for it's protected by bosses, plates, and brass clasps.

Polyphemus. Take a good look at it.

Cannius. I'm looking. Very fine, but you haven't yet decorated it enough.

Polyphemus. What's lacking?

Cannius. You should have added your coat of arms.

Polyphemus. What coat of arms?

Cannius. The head of Silenus [3] peering out of a wine jug. But what's the book about? The art of drinking?

Polyphemus. Be careful you don't blurt out blasphemy.

Cannius. What, you don't mean it's something sacred?

Polyphemus. The most sacred of all, the Gospels.

Cannius. By Hercules! What has Polyphemus to do with the Gospels?

Polyphemus. You might as well ask what a Christian has to do with Christ.

Cannius. I'm not sure a halberd isn't more fitting for the likes of you. If I were at sea and met a stranger who looked like this, I'd take him for a pirate; if I met him in a wood, for a bandit.

Polyphemus. Yet this very Gospel teaches us not to judge a man by appearances. Just as a haughty spirit often lurks under an ash-colored cowl, so a cropped head, curled beard, stern brow, wild eyes, plumed cap, military cloak, and slashed breeches sometimes cover a true Christian heart.

Cannius. Of course. Sometimes a sheep lurks in wolf's clothing, too. And if you trust fables, an ass in a lion's skin.

Polyphemus. What's more, I know a man who has a sheep's head and a fox's heart. I could wish him friends as fair as his eyes are dark, and a character as shining as his complexion.[4]

3 In Greek mythology, a drunken Satyr.

4 This passage embarrassed Erasmus when it was interpreted as a libel

Cannius. If a man with a sheepskin cap has a sheep's head, what a load *you* carry, with both a sheep and an ostrich on your head.[5] And isn't it rather ridiculous to have a bird on your head and an ass in your heart?

Polyphemus. That hurt!

Cannius. But it would be well if, as you've decorated the Gospels with various ornaments, the Gospels in turn adorned you. You've decorated them with colors; I wish they might embellish you with good morals.[6]

Polyphemus. I'll take care of that.

Cannius. After your fashion, yes.

Polyphemus. But insults aside, you don't condemn those who carry a volume of the Gospels about, do you?

Cannius. I'd be the last person in the world to do that.

Polyphemus. What? I seem to you the least person in the world, when I'm taller than you by an ass's head?

Cannius. I don't believe you'd be that much taller even if the ass pricked up its ears.

Polyphemus. Certainly by a buffalo's.

Cannius. I like the comparison. But I said "last"; I wasn't calling you "least."

Polyphemus. What's the difference between an egg and an egg?

Cannius. What's the difference between middle finger and little finger?

---

on Johannes Oecolampadius, a former friend who had joined the Reformers and was now one of the leaders of the Reformation in Switzerland. (In the first edition the passage had a sentence about the man's long nose, but these words were omitted in the next edition.) Erasmus' explanation, which Oecolampadius accepted, was that he was joking about Cannius, who fitted the description. Reformation, however, had made life in Basel so turbulent by this time that Erasmus determined to leave. In April, 1529, a month after the publication of this colloquy, he migrated to Freiburg in the Breisgau, where he remained for six years.

5 Soldiers commonly wore tall plumes in their helmets or caps.

6 Erasmus says in a letter that "Polyphemus used to carry about with him a beautifully decorated volume of the Gospels, although nothing could be more soiled than his own life" (*Erasmi Epistolae*, VIII, 135. 18-20).

Polyphemus. The middle one's longer.

Cannius. Very good! What's the difference between ass ears and wolf ears?

Polyphemus. Wolf ears are shorter.

Cannius. That's right.

Polyphemus. But I'm in the habit of measuring long and short by span and ell, not by ears.

Cannius. Well, the man who carried Christ was called Christopher. You, who carry the Gospels, ought to be called Gospel-bearer instead of Polyphemus.

Polyphemus. Don't you think it's holy to carry the Gospels?

Cannius. No—unless you'd agree that asses are mighty holy.

Polyphemus. How so?

Cannius. Because one of them can carry three thousand books of this kind. I should think you'd be equal to that load if fitted with the right packsaddle.

Polyphemus. There's nothing farfetched in thus crediting an ass with holiness because he carried Christ.

Cannius. I don't envy you that holiness. And if you like, I'll give you relics of the ass that carried Christ, so you can kiss them.

Polyphemus. A gift I'll be glad to get. For by touching the body of Christ that ass was consecrated.

Cannius. Obviously those who smote Christ touched him too.

Polyphemus. But tell me seriously, isn't carrying the Gospel about a reverent thing to do?

Cannius. Reverent if done sincerely, without hypocrisy.

Polyphemus. Let monks have hypocrisy! What has a soldier to do with hypocrisy?

Cannius. But first tell me what hypocrisy is.

Polyphemus. Professing something other than what you really mean.

Cannius. But what does carrying a copy of the Gospels profess? A gospel life, doesn't it?

Polyphemus. I suppose so.

Cannius. Therefore, when the life doesn't correspond to the book, isn't that hypocrisy?

Polyphemus. Apparently. But what is it truly to bear the Gospel?

Cannius. Some bear it in their hands, as the Franciscans do their Rule. Parisian porters, and asses and geldings, can do the same. There are those who bear it in their mouths, harping on nothing but Christ and the Gospel. That's pharisaical. Some bear it in their hearts. The true Gospel bearer, then, is one who carries it in hands and mouth *and* heart.

Polyphemus. Where are these?

Cannius. In churches—the deacons, who bear the book, read it to the congregation, and have it by heart.

Polyphemus. Though not all who bear the Gospel in their hearts are devout.

Cannius. Don't quibble. A man doesn't bear it in his heart unless he loves it through and through. Nobody loves it wholeheartedly unless he emulates the Gospel in his manner of living.

Polyphemus. I don't follow these subtleties.

Cannius. But I'll tell you more bluntly. If you carry a jar of Beaune wine [7] on your shoulder, it's just a burden, isn't it?

Polyphemus. That's all.

Cannius. But if you hold the wine in your throat, and presently spit it out?

Polyphemus. Useless—though, really, I'm not accustomed to doing that!

Cannius. But if—as you *are* accustomed—you take a long drink?

Polyphemus. Nothing more heavenly.

Cannius. Your whole body glows; your face turns rosy; your expression grows merry.

Polyphemus. Exactly.

Cannius. The Gospel has the same effect when it penetrates the heart. It makes a new man of you.

[7] A kind of Burgundy that Erasmus preferred above all other wines.

Polyphemus. So I don't seem to you to live according to the Gospel?

Cannius. You can best decide that question yourself.

Polyphemus. If it could be decided with a battle-ax—

Cannius. If someone called you a liar or a rake to your face, what would you do?

Polyphemus. What would I do? He'd feel my fists.

Cannius. What if someone hit you hard?

Polyphemus. I'd break his neck for that.

Cannius. But your book teaches you to repay insults with a soft answer; and "Whosoever shall smite thee on thy right cheek, turn to him the other also." [8]

Polyphemus. I've read that, but it slipped my mind.

Cannius. You pray frequently, I dare say.

Polyphemus. That's pharisaical.

Cannius. Long-winded but ostentatious praying is pharisaical. But your book teaches us to pray without ceasing,[9] yet sincerely.

Polyphemus. Still, I do pray sometimes.

Cannius. When?

Polyphemus. Whenever I think of it—once or twice a week.

Cannius. What do you pray?

Polyphemus. The Lord's Prayer.

Cannius. How often?

Polyphemus. Once. For the Gospel forbids vain repetitions as "much speaking." [10]

Cannius. Can you concentrate on the Lord's Prayer while repeating it?

Polyphemus. Never tried. Isn't it enough to say the words?

Cannius. I don't know, except that God hears only the utterance of the heart. Do you fast often?

Polyphemus. Never.

Cannius. But your book recommends prayer and fasting.

8 Matthew 5:39.
9 I Thessalonians 5:17.
10 Matthew 6:7.

Polyphemus. I'd recommend them too, if my belly did not demand something else.

Cannius. But Paul says that those who serve their bellies aren't serving Jesus Christ.[11] Do you eat meat on any day whatever?

Polyphemus. Any day it's offered.

Cannius. Yet a man as tough as you are could live on hay or the bark of trees.

Polyphemus. But Christ said that a man is not defiled by what he eats.[12]

Cannius. True, if it's eaten in moderation, without giving offense. But Paul, the disciple of Christ, prefers starvation to offending a weak brother by his food; [13] and he calls upon us to follow his example, in order that we may please all men in all things.

Polyphemus. Paul's Paul, and I'm me [*ego*].

Cannius. But Egon's job is to feed she-goats.[14]

Polyphemus. I'd rather eat one.

Cannius. A fine wish! You'll be a billygoat rather than a she-goat.

Polyphemus. I said *eat* one, not *be* one.

Cannius. Very prettily said. Are you generous to the poor?

Polyphemus. I've nothing to give.

Cannius. But you would have, if you lived soberly and worked hard.

Polyphemus. I'm fond of loafing.

Cannius. Do you keep God's commandments?

Polyphemus. That's tiresome.

Cannius. Do you do penance for your sins?

Polyphemus. Christ has paid for us.

Cannius. Then why do you insist you love the Gospel?

Polyphemus. I'll tell you. A certain Franciscan in our neighborhood kept babbling from the pulpit against Erasmus'

11 Romans 16:18.
12 Mark 7:15.
13 I Corinthians 6:12-13, 10:25-28.
14 Virgil, *Eclogues,* iii, 1-2.

New Testament. I met the man privately, grabbed him by the hair with my left hand, and punched him with my right. I gave him a hell of a beating; made his whole face swell. What do you say to that? Isn't that promoting the Gospel? Next I gave him absolution by banging him on the head three times with this very same book, raising three lumps, in the name of Father, Son, and Holy Ghost.

Cannius. The evangelical spirit, all right! This is certainly defending the Gospel with the Gospel.

Polyphemus. I ran across another member of the same order who never stopped raving against Erasmus.[15] Fired with evangelical zeal, I threatened the fellow so much he begged pardon on both knees and admitted the devil had put him up to saying what he said. If he hadn't done this, my halberd would have bounced against his head. I looked as fierce as Mars in battle. This took place before witnesses.

Cannius. I'm surprised the man didn't drop dead on the spot. But let's go on. Do you live chastely?

Polyphemus. I may when I'm old. But shall I confess the truth to you, Cannius?

Cannius. I'm no priest. If you want to confess, find somebody else.

Polyphemus. Usually I confess to God, but to you I admit I'm not yet a perfect follower of the Gospel; just an ordinary fellow. My kind have four Gospels. Four things above all we Gospelers seek: full bellies; plenty of work for the organs below the belly; a livelihood from somewhere or other; finally, freedom to do as we please. If we get these, we shout in our cups, "Io, triumph; Io, Paean! The Gospel flourishes! Christ reigns!"

Cannius. That's an Epicurean life, surely, not an evangelical one.

---

15 One of these Franciscans may be Francis Titelmans, a Louvain theologian who had recently attacked Erasmus. The passage may allude also to a recent altercation between Polyphemus and Louis Carinus, a former pupil of Erasmus who was now at odds with him. Cf. *Erasmi Epistolae,* VIII, 71. 28 n.; 72. 31-33.

Polyphemus. I don't deny it, but you know Christ is omnipotent and can turn us into other men in the twinkling of an eye.

Cannius. Into swine, too, which I think is more likely than into good men.

Polyphemus. I wish there were no worse creatures in the world than swine, oxen, asses, and camels! You can meet many men who are fiercer than lions, greedier than wolves, more lecherous than sparrows, more snappish than dogs, more venomous than vipers.

Cannius. But now it's time for you to begin changing from brute to man.

Polyphemus. You do well to warn me, for prophets [16] these days declare the end of the world is at hand.

Cannius. All the more reason to hurry.

Polyphemus. I await the hand of Christ.

Cannius. See that you are pliant material for his hand! But where do they get the notion that the end of the world is near?

Polyphemus. They say it's because men are behaving now just as they did before the Flood overwhelmed them. They feast, drink, stuff themselves, marry and are given in marriage, whore, buy, sell, pay and charge interest, build buildings. Kings make war, priests are zealous to increase their wealth, theologians invent syllogisms, monks roam through the world, the commons riot, Erasmus writes colloquies. In short, no calamity is lacking: hunger, thirst, robbery, war, plague, sedition, poverty. Doesn't this prove human affairs are at an end?

Cannius. In this mass of woes, what worries you most?

Polyphemus. Guess.

Cannius. That your purse is full of cobwebs.[17]

Polyphemus. Damned if you haven't hit it! —Just now I'm on my way back from a drinking party. Some other time,

[16] Some of the Anabaptist leaders of the 1520s had predicted the imminent end of the world. Cf. *Erasmi Epistolae,* VIII, 137. 5—138. 20.

[17] Catullus, xiii, 7-8.

when I'm more sober, I'll argue with you about the Gospel, if you like.

Cannius. When shall I see you sober?

Polyphemus. When I'm sober.

Cannius. When will you be so?

Polyphemus. When you see me so. Meantime, my dear Cannius, good luck.

Cannius. I hope you, in turn, become what you're called.

Polyphemus. To prevent you from outdoing me in courtesy, I pray that Cannius, as the name implies, may never be lacking a can!

❧ X ❧

THE GODLY FEAST

A few pages of this colloquy—merely the introductory material—appeared in the March, 1522, edition; the rest in a later edition of 1522. In the later edition the names of five speakers were changed: Adolphus, Balbus, Cornelius, Durandus, and Everardus became Eusebius, Timotheus, Theophilus, Chrysoglottus, and Uranius. They have not been identified (for some guesses, see Preserved Smith, *A Key to the Colloquies of Erasmus*, 1927, p. 11).

Although gardens and country houses were conventional settings for dialogues in Renaissance as in classical literature, the villa in "The Godly Feast," with its frescoes of Christian and pagan subjects, resembles somewhat an actual house known to Erasmus: that of his friend Johannes von Botzheim, Canon of Constance. Erasmus visited Botzheim in September, 1522, and in a letter written some months later described the house (*Erasmi Epistolae*, V, 212. 335-354). Possibly the enlarged text of this colloquy was composed after September; we do not know exactly when in 1522 the later edition appeared. Very likely there are also recollections here of the country house at Anderlecht, near Brussels, where Erasmus lived agreeably from May to November, 1521.

In its exegesis of Scripture, sentiments on the Christian life, and judgments of the virtuous ancients—a famous passage—this is a characteristic Erasmian dialogue.

EUSEBIUS, TIMOTHY, THEOPHILUS, CHRYSOGLOTTUS, URANIUS
[SOPHRONIUS, EULALIUS, NEPHALIUS, THEODIDACTUS,
SERVANT BOY]

Eusebius. Now that the whole countryside is fresh and smiling, I marvel at people who take pleasure in smoky cities.

Timothy. Some people don't enjoy the sight of flowers or verdant meadows or fountains or streams; or if they do, something else pleases them more. Thus pleasure succeeds pleasure, as nail drives out nail.

Eusebius. Maybe you're referring to moneylenders, or greedy merchants, who are just like them.

Timothy. Those, yes, but not those alone, my good friend. No, countless others besides them, including the very priests and monks themselves, who for the sake of gain usually prefer to live in cities—the most populous cities. They follow not Pythagorean or Platonic doctrine, but that of a certain blind beggar who rejoiced in the jostling of a crowd, because (he said) where there were people, there was his profit.

Eusebius. Away with the blind and their profit! We are philosophers.

Timothy. Also the philosopher Socrates [1] preferred cities to fields, because he was eager to learn, and cities afforded him means of learning. In the fields, to be sure, were trees and gardens, fountains and streams, that pleased the eye; but they had nothing to say, and therefore taught nothing.

Eusebius. Socrates wasn't altogether wrong, if you mean roaming in the fields by yourself. In my opinion, however, Nature is not silent but talks to us all the time, on every hand, and teaches the observant man many things if she finds him attentive and receptive. What else does the charming countenance of blooming Nature proclaim than that God the creator's wisdom is equal to his goodness? But how many things does Socrates teach his Phaedrus in that retreat, and how many learn from him in turn!

Timothy. If people of that sort were present, nothing could be more enjoyable than country life.

Eusebius. Then would you care to chance this? I've a little villa outside of town, a small but well-cultivated place, to which I invite you for lunch tomorrow.

Timothy. There are a good many of us. We'd eat you out of house and home.

Eusebius. Oh, no, you'll have a green feast made, as Hor-

[1] *Phaedrus,* 230b-e.

ace [2] says, "from food not bought." The place itself supplies the wine; the very trees all but drop pumpkins, melons, figs, pears, apples, and nuts into your lap, as happens (if we believe Lucian) [3] in the Fortunate Isles. Perhaps we can have a hen from the coop.

Timothy. Well, we don't decline.

Eusebius. But let each one bring his shadow [4] along if he likes. Thus, since there are four of you, we'll equal the number of the Muses.

Timothy. We'll do it.

Eusebius. But I must warn you of one thing: everybody should bring his own seasoning with him. I'll furnish only the food.

Timothy. What seasoning do you mean, pepper or sugar?

Eusebius. No, something commoner but more agreeable.

Timothy. What?

Eusebius. An appetite. A light supper today will take care of that. Tomorrow a walk will sharpen it; and my little country place will furnish the walk, too. What hour do you like for lunch?

Timothy. About ten, before the heat's too great.

Eusebius. I'll arrange it.

Boy. Master, the guests are at the gate.

Eusebius. You're as good as your word about coming, but it's doubly gratifying that you've come early, along with your shadows, who are most welcome. For there are ill-bred guests who torment a host by being late.

Timothy. We came earlier in order to have time to walk round and see this palace of yours, which we hear is filled with various delights—not a corner that doesn't bear the master's stamp.

Eusebius. You'll see a palace worthy of such a king. To

2 *Epodes,* ii, 48.
3 In his *True History,* ii, 13-14.
4 I.e., a companion.

me, certainly, it is a little nest dearer than any palace. And if he may be said to reign who lives exactly as he pleases, clearly I reign here. But it's best, I think, while the queen of the kitchen prepares a salad, and while the heat of the sun is still moderate, to visit my gardens.

Timothy. There's another besides this? For this admirably tended one immediately greets those entering it with the most delightful spectacle, and receives them cordially.

Eusebius. Then let everyone pick some blossoms and leaves from it, so the squalor of the house won't give offense. The same scent is not pleasing to everyone; therefore let each one of you choose for himself. Don't be sparing, for I allow whatever grows here to be almost public property. The door of this courtyard is never shut except at night.

Timothy. Look, here's Peter at the door.

Eusebius. I'd rather have him as porter than the Mercuries, Centaurs, and other monsters some people paint on their doors.

Timothy. This is more appropriate to a Christian.

Eusebius. My doorkeeper's no silent one, either. He greets the caller in three languages.

Timothy. What does he say?

Eusebius. Why not read it for yourself?

Timothy. It's a little too far away for me to make out plainly.

Eusebius. Here's a magnifying glass that will make you a Lynceus.

Timothy. I see the Latin: "If thou wilt enter into life, keep the commandments."

Eusebius. Now read the Greek.

Timothy. I see the Greek all right, but it's Greek to me, so I'll hand the torch to Theophilus, who's always spouting Greek.

Theophilus. "Repent ye, therefore, and be converted."

Chrysoglottus. I'll take the Hebrew: "The just shall live by his faith." [5]

[5] Matthew 19:17; Acts 3:19; Habakkuk 2:4.

Eusebius. Does he seem to you an uncivil porter, who at one and the same time warns us to avoid sin and turn to the pursuit of godliness; next, warns us that we do not attain to the true Christian life by works of the Mosaic law, but through gospel faith; finally, that the way to life eternal is by obeying the commandments of the Gospel?

Timothy. And look: the passage on the right shows us presently an exquisite little chapel. On the altar Jesus Christ gazes heavenward, whence his Father and the Holy Spirit look out, and he points to heaven with his right hand while with his left he seems to invite and allure the passerby.

Eusebius. Nor does he receive us in silence: you see in Latin, "I am the way, and the truth, and the life"; in Greek, "I am Alpha and Omega"; and in Hebrew, "Come, ye children, hearken unto me; I will teach you the fear of the Lord." [6]

Timothy. Truly the Lord Jesus has greeted us with glad tidings.

Eusebius. But lest we seem rude, perhaps we should return his greeting. Let us pray that since we can avail nothing of ourselves, he in his infinite goodness may never let us stray from the path of salvation; but, after we have rejected Jewish forms and the deceits of this world, may guide us through gospel truth to life eternal—that is, draw us to himself by himself.

Timothy. A quite reasonable proposal; and the very appearance of the place invites one to pray.

Eusebius. The charm of this garden entices many guests, but so strong is the force of custom that hardly any of them passes Jesus without greeting him. I've placed him here, instead of the filthy Priapus,[7] as protector not only of my garden but of everything I own; in short, of body and soul alike. Here, as you see, is a little fountain bubbling merrily with excellent water. It symbolizes in a manner that unique fountain

6 John 14:6; Revelation 1:8; Psalms 34:11.

7 A fertility god, protector of vineyards and gardens.

which refreshes with its heavenly stream all those who labor and are heavy laden, and for which the soul, wearied by the evils of this world, pants, as, according to the Psalmist, does the thirsty hart after tasting the flesh of serpents.[8] Whoever thirsts is welcome to drink of it. And some for religion's sake sprinkle themselves with the water. Some even drink, not because of thirst, but of religion.

I see you don't like to be torn away from this spot, but meantime the hour warns us to visit the more cultivated garden that the walls of my palace enclose in a square. If there's anything to be seen in the house, you'll view it after lunch, when the sun's heat will keep us at home like snails for some hours.

Timothy. Oh! I seem to behold Epicurean gardens.

Eusebius. This entire place is intended for pleasure—honest pleasure, that is: to feast the eyes, refresh the nostrils, restore the soul. Only fragrant herbs grow here, and those not just any herbs, but only choice ones. Each kind has its own beds.

Timothy. Your herbs here aren't speechless, either, so far as I can see.

Eusebius. Quite right. Other men have luxurious homes; I have one where there's a great deal of talk, that I may never seem lonely. You'll say so even more emphatically when you've seen the whole thing. As the herbs are gathered into companies, so to speak, so each company has its banner, with an inscription. For instance, the marjoram here says "Keep off, sow; I don't smell for you," because swine positively hate this odor, although it is the sweetest of scents. Each kind likewise has its own label indicating the special virtue of that herb.

Timothy. Thus far I've seen nothing more agreeable than this little fountain. Here in their midst it seems to smile on all the herbs, and promises to keep them cool in the heat. But this narrow channel which shows all the water so gracefully to

[8] Cf. Psalms 41:2. ". . . after tasting the flesh of serpents" is not in the received text of the psalm.

men's eyes, dividing the garden on either side in equal distances, and in which all its herbs are reflected as though in a mirror—is it made of marble?

Eusebius. Mind what you're saying! Where would marble come from? It's imitation marble made of cement, with a coating of white paint added.

Timothy. Where does such a pretty stream finally bury itself?

Eusebius. See how crude we are: after it has delighted our eyes here sufficiently, it drains the kitchen and carries that waste along to the sewer.

Timothy. That's callous, so help me!

Eusebius. Callous, unless God's goodness had made it for this use. We're callous, too, when we pollute with our sins and wicked lusts the fountain of Sacred Scripture—a far more pleasing fountain than this, given to refresh as well as cleanse our souls—and misuse so unspeakable a gift of God. We do not misuse this water if we employ it for the various purposes for which it was given by Him who provides abundantly for human needs.

Timothy. What you say is very true. But why are even your artificial hedges green?

Eusebius. In order that there might be nothing here that isn't green. Some people prefer red because that color enhances green things. I prefer this. Every man to his taste, even in gardens.

Timothy. The garden by itself is charming, but its beauty is almost overshadowed by the three galleries.

Eusebius. In these I study or stroll, conversing with myself or some close friend. Or, if the fancy strikes me, I have a meal here.

Timothy. Those evenly spaced pillars that support the building, so fascinating by their marvelous variety of colors— are *they* marble?

Eusebius. The same marble this channel is made of.

Timothy. An artistic deception indeed! I'd have sworn they were marble.

Eusebius. Let that be a warning to you not to believe or swear to anything rashly: appearances often deceive. We make up for lack of wealth by ingenuity.

[*They turn now to the frescoes on the walls of the galleries.*]

Timothy. Wasn't so neat and trim a garden good enough for you unless you painted other ones besides?

Eusebius. One garden wasn't enough to hold all kinds of plants. Moreover, we are twice pleased when we see a painted flower competing with a real one. In one we admire the cleverness of Nature, in the other the inventiveness of the painter; in each the goodness of God, who gives all these things for our use and is equally wonderful and kind in everything. Finally, a garden isn't always green, nor flowers always blooming. This garden grows and pleases even in midwinter.

Timothy. Yet it doesn't breathe.

Eusebius. But on the other hand it needs no attention.

Timothy. It pleases only the eyes.

Eusebius. True, but it does that forever.

Timothy. A picture, too, grows old.

Eusebius. Yes, but it's longer-lived than we are, and age commonly adds to it a grace we lose.

Timothy. I wish you were wrong about that!

Eusebius. In this gallery, which faces west, I enjoy the morning sun; in that one, which looks to the east, I sun myself sometimes; in the one which looks south but lies open to the north, I take refuge from the heat. Let's walk around, if you like, to get a better view. See, the very ground is green; the paving stones, too, are beautifully colored, and gladden one with painted flowers. This painted grove you observe, covering the entire wall, presents a varied spectacle. In the first place, you see as many varieties of trees as you do trees, each one represented with no little accuracy. You see as many species of birds as you do birds, especially those that are rather rare and renowned for one reason or another. (What use to paint geese, hens, and ducks?) Underneath are species of quadrupeds, or of those birds that live on the ground like quadrupeds.

Timothy. A wonderful variety, and nothing inactive, nothing that's not doing or saying something. What does the owl, almost hidden under the branches, tell us?

Eusebius. An Attic owl, it speaks the Attic tongue: [9] "Be prudent: I don't fly for everyone." It bids us act advisedly, because unadvised rashness sometimes brings misfortune. Here an eagle rends a hare, a beetle protesting in vain. Beside the beetle stands a wren, the deadly enemy of the eagle.

Timothy. What does the swallow carry in its mouth?

Eusebius. Swallowwort, for by this she restores the sight of her blind fledglings. Do you recognize that plant?

Timothy. What new kind of lizard is this?

Eusebius. It's not a lizard but a chameleon.

Timothy. Is this the chameleon I've heard so much about? I thought it was a bigger beast than a lion, whom it surpasses even in name.

Eusebius. This chameleon here is always openmouthed, always hungry. Here's a wild fig tree. Only when near it is he fierce; at other times he's harmless. But he does have poison; don't scorn a gaping creature so small.

Timothy. But he isn't changing his color.

Eusebius. True, because he isn't changing his place; when he changes his place you'll see a different color.

Timothy. What's the piper doing here?

Eusebius. Don't you see the camel dancing nearby?

Timothy. I see a strange sight: a wanton camel, and a monkey for his piper.

Eusebius. But there'll be opportunity to examine these sights one by one at your leisure some other time, or for three days together. Enough now to have seen them as if through a

---

[9] Because sacred to Pallas Athene. Most of the numerous proverbs and many of the allusions to natural history in this colloquy Erasmus explicates in his *Adagia*, a collection of aphorisms with comments or essays. First published in 1500 and often reprinted, it was an extremely popular book throughout the sixteenth century.

lattice. Over here is every kind of famous plant accurately painted, and (what you may well wonder at), however instantly poisonous they are, here they may not only be viewed safely but even touched.

Timothy. Here's a scorpion, a rare pest in these parts but common in Italy. Though to me his color in the picture doesn't seem convincing.

Eusebius. How so?

Timothy. Because the Italian ones are darker: this one's rather light.

Eusebius. But don't you recognize the plant he's fallen on?

Timothy. Not well enough.

Eusebius. No wonder, for it doesn't grow in our gardens. It's wolfsbane, so poisonous that when a scorpion comes in contact with it he's stunned, turns pale, and surrenders. But, injured by a poison, he seeks a remedy in poison. You see nearby every variety of hellebore. If the scorpion can get free of the wolfsbane leaf and touch the white hellebore, he'll recover his old strength; the touch of a different poison cures his numbness.

Timothy. Then this scorpion's done for, because he'll never free himself from the wolfsbane leaf.—Do even scorpions talk here?

Eusebius. Yes, and in Greek, too.

Timothy. What does he say?

Eusebius. "God hath found out the guilty." Here beside the herbs you see every kind of serpent. Look, a basilisk, dreadful with his fiery eyes and extremely dangerous poisons.

Timothy. He, too, is saying something.

Eusebius. "Let them hate, so long as they fear."

Timothy. A royal saying, clearly.

Eusebius. No, nothing is less royal; the saying of a tyrant, rather. Here a lizard fights with an adder. Here a dipsas lurks, hidden by the shell of an ostrich egg. Here you see a whole republic of ants, whom the Hebrew sage [10] urges us to imitate;

[10] Proverbs 6:6.

and so does our Horace,[11] too. Here you see Indian ants, which carry gold and hoard it.

Timothy. Good heavens, who could possibly get bored in this changing scene?

Eusebius. At some other time, I say, you may look at it until you're tired. For the present, just observe the third wall from a distance. It has lakes, rivers, and seas, containing every kind of famous fish. Here's the Nile, in which you see the dolphin, who loves men, fighting with a crocodile, than whom man has no deadlier enemy. On the banks you see amphibians, such as crabs, seals, a beaver. Here's a polypus, a captor captured by an oyster.

Timothy. What's the inscription? "The captor captive." The painter has made the water wonderfully clear.

Eusebius. He had to, or we should have needed other eyes. Next is another polypus, sailing merrily along the surface like a yacht. You see a torpedo lying on sand of the same color; here you can touch it safely with your hand. But we must hurry on to another place. These sights feast the eyes but don't fill the belly. Let's get on to the rest.

Timothy. Still more?

Eusebius. You'll soon see what the back door has to show us. Here you see an ample garden, divided into two parts. In one are herbs for the table; my wife and maidservant rule here. In the other are all sorts of medicinal herbs, especially the rare ones. To the left is an open meadow with nothing but green grass, and enclosed by a continuous hedge of hawthorn. There I stroll sometimes or entertain myself with company. To the right is an orchard in which, at your leisure, you'll see many exotic trees. These I'm gradually training to accustom themselves to our climate.

Timothy. Well! You outdo Alcinous [12] himself.

Eusebius. Here at the end, joining the upper gallery, which you'll see after lunch, is an aviary. You'll see different

11 *Sat.,* I, i, 32-35.
12 *Odyssey,* vi-vii.

shapes and hear different tongues. No less different are the birds' natures: among some, kinship and mutual affection; among others, irreconcilable enmity. Yet they're all so tame that when the window there is opened at dinner, they fly down to the table and take food from your hands. Whenever I approach on the little arched bridge you see, talking with a friend, they sit nearby and listen, perching on my arms or shoulders, so fearless are they, because they know nobody harms them. At the far end of the orchard is the kingdom of the bees; no unattractive sight, either. I won't let you look any more just now; I want you to have something to bring you back, as though to a new spectacle. After lunch I'll show you the rest.

Boy. Your wife and the maid insist lunch is getting spoiled.

Eusebius. Tell them to be calm, we're coming right away. Let's wash, gentlemen, that we may approach the table with hands and hearts both clean. For truly if a meal was a holy thing to pagans, much more should it be so to Christians, for whom it's an allegory of that sacred last supper which the Lord Jesus had with his disciples. Hence the custom of washing the hands, in order that if perchance any hatred, envy, or shamefulness dwell in one's mind, he may get rid of it before coming to eat. And indeed I believe food is better for the body if eaten with a pure mind.

Timothy. We heartily agree.

Eusebius. Since Christ himself set the example of hallowing the food by a hymn—for I believe we often read in the Gospel that he blessed food or gave thanks to his Father before breaking bread—and again of ending with a hymn, I'll recite, if you like, a hymn that St. Chrysostom praises very highly in one of his homilies and even thought worthy of a commentary.[13]

Timothy. We beg you to do so.

Eusebius. "Blessed be thou, O God, who hast nourished

[13] *Homilies on Matthew,* 55. Erasmus edited and translated some of Chrysostom's works.

me from my youth up, who providest food for every creature. Fill our hearts with joy and gladness, that having abundance we may abound to every good work. In the name of Christ Jesus our Lord, to whom with thee and the Holy Spirit be glory, honor, and dominion forever."

Timothy. Amen.

Eusebius. Now sit down, every one with his shadow. Timothy, your gray hairs entitle you to be at the head of the table.

Timothy. You've expressed my whole merit in a word. On this score alone am I to be preferred before the others.

Eusebius. God is the judge of other gifts; we go by what we see. Sophronius, stay where you are. Theophilus and Eulalius, sit at the right of the table. Chrysoglottus and Theodidactus will take the left, Uranius and Nephalius the other places. I'll guard this corner.

Timothy. We won't allow that. The host should be at the head of the table.

Eusebius. What's mine here is yours too, but if I may have authority in my own realm, I decree that the host is to have whichever place he chooses. Now may Christ, who makes all men to rejoice, and without whom nothing is truly pleasing, deign to attend our feast and rejoice our hearts by his presence.

Timothy. I hope he will deign to do so. But since every place is filled, where will he sit?

Eusebius. May he mingle with all our food and drink, so that everything taste of him, but most of all may he penetrate our minds! That he may please to come, and we make ourselves the readier for so great a guest, you shall hear (if you don't object) a short passage from Sacred Scripture, but in such fashion that this won't interfere with your eating eggs and lettuce if you like.

Timothy. We'll eat with pleasure, but listen with even more pleasure.

Eusebius. This custom, it seems to me, has much to recommend it, because by means of it we avoid foolish yarns and enjoy profitable conversation.[14] I disagree emphatically with those who think a dinner party isn't fun unless it overflows with silly, bawdy stories and rings with dirty songs. True gaiety comes from a clean, sincere conscience. And truly enjoyable conversations are those which are always pleasant to have held or heard, and always delightful to recall, not those which soon cause one to be ashamed and conscience-stricken.

Timothy. Would that we all weighed these words as much as their truth deserves!

Eusebius. Besides being certain, and eminently useful, they're pleasant when you've been accustomed to them for a month.

Timothy. Nothing is more advisable, therefore, than to habituate ourselves to excellence.

Eusebius. Read clearly and distinctly, boy.

Boy. "The king's heart is in the hand of the Lord, as the rivers of water: he turneth it whithersoever he will. Every way of a man is right in his own eyes; but the Lord pondereth the hearts. To do justice and judgment is more acceptable to the Lord than sacrifice." [15]

Eusebius. That will do. For it's more profitable to learn a few things eagerly than to swallow many in boredom.

Timothy. Very true, but not of this book only. Pliny [16] writes that Cicero's *De Officiis* should never be out of one's hands, and in my opinion it certainly deserves the closest study by everyone, especially by those destined for careers in government. But this little book of Proverbs I've always considered worthy of being carried with us at all times.

Eusebius. I've provided it as seasoning, since I knew the lunch would be thin and insipid.

Timothy. Really, it's all very delightful; and yet if we

[14] Erasmus records elsewhere that Dean Colet had a passage from Proverbs or Paul's epistles read at supper, and then discussed by the guests (*Erasmi Epistolae*, IV, 516. 312-318).

[15] Proverbs 21:1-3.

[16] *Natural History*, preface, xxii-xxiii.

had nothing but beets without pepper, wine, and vinegar, such a reading would season everything.

Eusebius. Nevertheless I should be better pleased if I understood thoroughly what I heard. I wish we had here a good theologian who not only understood these matters but had taste as well. I don't know whether it's permissible for us laymen to discuss these topics.

Timothy. Permissible even for sailors, in my opinion, provided they're cautious about passing judgment. And perhaps Christ, who promised to be present wherever two men gathered in his name, will help us, since we are so many.

Eusebius. Then suppose we divide the three verses among us nine?

Guests. Good. Only let the host begin.

Eusebius. I wouldn't decline my appointment, but I'm afraid the fare I provide may be even worse than the food I serve you. All right; I don't want to be a disagreeable host. Putting aside the various conjectures of the commentators on this passage, I think its moral sense is this. Other mortals can be swayed by warnings, scoldings, laws, and threats; the king's heart, if you oppose it, is annoyed rather, since it *fears* nobody. And therefore, whenever princes have their minds set on anything they should be left to their whims, not because they always desire what is best, but because God sometimes uses their madness or wickedness to correct sinners, as he forbade resistance to Nebuchadnezzar because he had decided to chastise his people through the agency of this king.[17] Perhaps that is what Job means: "Who maketh the hypocrite reign for the sins of the people." [18] And maybe what David says, lamenting his sin, applies here: "Against thee, thee only, have I sinned, and done this evil in thy sight." [19] Not that kings don't commit sin, to the great injury of their subjects, but no subject has authority to condemn kings; whereas no one, be he ever so mighty, can escape God's judgment.

17 Jeremiah 27.
18 Job 34:30 (Vulgate).
19 Psalms 51:4.

Timothy. Your interpretation does not displease me. But what does "the rivers of water" mean?

Eusebius. There's a comparison at hand to explain it. A king's mind, when aroused, is violent and unrestrained; it cannot be led this way or that but is driven by its own force, as if excited by a divine frenzy, just as the sea spreads itself over the land and frequently changes course, heedless of fields, buildings, and whatever else stands in its way; in some places it goes underground. If you tried to stop its force or divert it, you could do nothing. The same with large rivers: witness stories about Achelous.[20] But you suffer less if you go along with the stream than if you resist violently.

Timothy. Then is there no remedy against the unbridled fury of wicked kings?

Eusebius. The first, perhaps, will be not to receive the lion into the city. Next, by authority of senate, magistrates, and people, to limit his power in such a way that he may not easily break out into tyranny. But the best safeguard of all is to shape his character by sacred teachings while he's still a boy and doesn't realize he's a ruler. Petitions and admonitions help, provided they are polite and temperate. Your last resource is to beseech God to incline the king's heart to conduct worthy of a Christian prince.

Timothy. What do you mean, "layman"? Were I a Bachelor of Theology, I'd be very little ashamed of this interpretation.

Eusebius. Whether it's correct, I don't know; I'm satisfied that the idea isn't irreverent or heretical. I've carried out your request. Now, as is proper at parties, it's my turn to hear you.

Timothy. I think—if you make allowance for these gray hairs—that this saying can be accommodated to a deeper meaning.

Eusebius. So do I, and I want to hear it.

Timothy. "King" can be understood as the perfect man who, with his bodily passions under control, is governed solely by the power of the Holy Spirit. Moreover, to compel such a

20 Ovid, *Met.*, viii, 549—ix, 100.

man to conform to human laws is perhaps unsuitable. Instead he should be left to his Master, by whose spirit he is led; he is not to be judged by those conditions through which the weak and simple are somehow drawn to true godliness. But if he does anything unrighteously, we ought to say with Paul, "God hath received him," "To his own master he standeth or falleth." [21] Likewise: "He that is spiritual judgeth all things, yet he himself is judged of no man." [22] Therefore nobody may prescribe to such men, but the Lord who set the bounds to sea and rivers has the heart of the king in his hand and directs it whithersoever he wills. For what need is there to prescribe for one who voluntarily exceeds the demands of human laws? Or what foolhardiness would it be to bind by human regulations the man who (as is evident by certain signs) is governed by the inspiration of the Holy Spirit? [23]

Eusebius. Truly, Timothy, you're venerable not in years only but in pure learning as well. And would that among Christians, all of whom should be kings, more such men might be found worthy of kingship!

But we've had enough of eggs and greens to start with. Have these removed and the other things served.

Timothy. I'm well satisfied with this "ovation" even if there's nothing else, either festival or triumph, to follow.

Eusebius. Yes, but since, by Christ's help as I believe, explication of the first sentence has been successful, I'd like your shadow to explain the second one, which seems to me somewhat more obscure.

Sophronius. If you'll take in good part whatever I say, I'll try my best to tell you how the matter looks to me. How else could a shadow shed light on darkness?

Eusebius. Well, on behalf of the company I accept the condition; and such shadows have their own light, one more suitable to our eyes.

[21] Romans 14:3-4.

[22] I Corinthians 2:15.

[23] This passage was censured by the Sorbonne (*Opera Omnia*, Leiden edition, IX, 934D—935B).

Sophronius. This doctrine seems the same as that of Paul, that piety is sought after by various modes of life. Some find the priesthood to their liking, some celibacy, some marriage, some retirement, some public affairs, according to their different constitutions and temperaments. Again, one man eats anything he likes; another discriminates between foods; another, between days; to another, every day is the same. In these matters Paul wants everyone to enjoy his own preference without reproach from anybody else. No man should judge in questions of this sort, but leave judgment to God, who pondereth the hearts. For it often happens that he who eats is more acceptable to God than he who does not; and he who profanes a holy day than he who seems to keep it; and this man's marriage is more acceptable in the sight of God than the celibacy of many others. I the shadow have had my say.

Eusebius. I hope it may often fall to my lot to talk with such shadows! Unless I'm mistaken, you've touched the spot, not, as they say, with the needle but with the tongue.—But here's one who's long lived celibate, yet is not of the company of the blessed who "have made themselves eunuchs for the kingdom of heaven's sake." [24] This creature was forcibly castrated to please the belly more, until "God shall destroy both it and meats." [25] It's a capon from my own coop. I'm fond of boiled dishes. The soup isn't bad; the lettuce swimming in it is very choice. Everybody help himself as he likes. But I don't wish to deceive you: we'll have a roast after this, then dessert, and finally the end of the story.

Timothy. But meantime we exclude your wife from the feast.

Eusebius. When you bring yours along, mine will sit down with us too. What would she be now but a mute? As a woman, she prefers to gossip with women; and we philosophize more freely. Otherwise we might run the risk of meeting with the same accident as befell Socrates. When he was entertaining philosophers—who would rather talk like this than eat—and

24 Matthew 19:12.
25 I Corinthians 6:13.

the argument went on and on, Xanthippe in a fit of anger upset the table.

Timothy. I'm sure there's nothing we need fear less from your wife, since she's a woman of very placid temper.

Eusebius. So much so to me, certainly, that I wouldn't exchange her if I could; and in this respect I account myself fortunate indeed. For I don't agree with those who think a man lucky not to have had a wife. I like rather the Hebrew sage's saying that "He that hath a good wife hath a good lot." [26]

Timothy. Often it's our own fault that our wives are bad, either because we choose bad ones, or make them such, or don't train and control them as we should.

Eusebius. Right. But meanwhile I'm waiting for an interpretation of the third sentence, and the inspired Theophilus, I think, is now ready to speak.

Theophilus. No, my mind was on my dishes. Nevertheless I'll speak, since I may do so safely.

Eusebius. You'll please us even by making a mistake, for thus you'll give us an opportunity of finding the right answer.

Theophilus. The idea seems to me the same as that which the Lord revealed through the prophet Hosea, Chapter 6: "I desire mercy, and not sacrifice; and the knowledge of God more than burnt offerings"; a passage whose living and effectual interpreter is the Lord Jesus in the Gospel of Matthew, Chapter 9. For when he would dine in the house of Levi the publican, who had invited many of his own class and occupation, the Pharisees—who vaunted themselves as strict keepers of the law, although they disregarded those commandments on which all the law and the prophets hung—in order to turn the minds of his disciples away from Jesus, asked them why their master ate with sinners, from whose company Jews abstained if they wanted to be considered especially holy; and if they chanced to meet such a person, took a bath as soon as they returned home. And since the disciples, still inexperienced, were at a loss to reply, the Lord answered for them as

[26] Proverbs 18:22 (Vulgate).

well as for himself: "They that be whole," he said, "need not a physician, but they that are sick. But go ye and learn what that meaneth, I will have mercy and not sacrifice: for I am not come to call the righteous but sinners to repentance." [27]

Eusebius. You explain the matter very well by comparing passages, an excellent method of biblical study. But I should like to learn what "sacrifice" and "mercy" mean. For how can God's rejection of sacrifices agree with his having commanded so often that they be made to him?

Theophilus. God himself teaches us in Isaiah 1 in what manner he rejects sacrifices. Jewish law enjoins some things that are expressions rather than proofs of holiness: such things as holy days, sabbaths, fasts, sacrifices. And there are some things always to be observed, things good not because they are commanded, but good *per se.* But God rejects the Jews, not because they would keep the rites of the law but because, foolishly puffed up by keeping them, they would neglect what God especially requires of us. Saturated with greed, pride, theft, hatred, envy, and other sins, they thought God much in their debt because they frequented the temple on holy days, offered burnt sacrifices, abstained from forbidden foods, and fasted occasionally. They embraced the shadows and neglected the substance. As for "I desire mercy and not sacrifice," I suppose this is Hebrew idiom for "I desire mercy *more than* sacrifice"; as Solomon means when he says, "To do justice and judgment is more acceptable to the Lord than sacrifice." [28] Moreover, every act of kindness done to help our neighbor the Scripture calls mercy and pity (the word "pity" is derived from "having mercy"). I think "sacrifice" means whatever pertains to corporeal rites and has some connection with Judaism, such as choice of foods, prescribed dress, fasting, sacrifice, perfunctory prayers, inactivity on holy days. Though not to be omitted entirely in certain seasons, these become displeasing to God if a person relies on such observances but neglects works of mercy when a brother's need calls for charity. To

27 Matthew 9:12-13.
28 Proverbs 21:3.

shun even the conversation of the wicked gives an appearance of holiness, but this should end as often as charity to a neighbor requires otherwise. To rest on holy days is obedience, but to let a brother perish on account of your religious observance of a day would be impious. Likewise I should say keeping the Sabbath is a sacrifice; to be reconciled with your brother, an act of mercy. Furthermore, although "judgment" can refer to rulers, who often oppress the weak by force, nevertheless I think it quite possibly agrees with what is said in Hosea: "And the knowledge of God more than burnt offerings." One does not keep the law unless he keeps it in accordance with God's purpose. The Jews rescued an ass if it fell into a ditch on the Sabbath, yet they reviled Christ for healing a man on the Sabbath. This was a preposterous judgment, and far from an understanding of God, for they did not realize that these institutions were made for man, not man for them.

But I might seem to say these things immodestly unless I said them by your command. I'd rather learn something more accurate from the others.

Eusebius. That was said so "immodestly" that for my part I could believe the Lord Jesus spoke through your mouth. But while we feast our minds plenteously, let not their partners be neglected.

Theophilus. Who are they?

Eusebius. Our bodies; aren't they partners of our minds? For I prefer "partners" to "instruments" or "dwellings" or "tombs."

Timothy. When the whole man is refreshed, this is abundant refreshment indeed.

Eusebius. I see you're slow to help yourselves, so with your permission I'll have the roast served, for fear I should give you a long feast instead of a luscious one. You behold the main course of our little luncheon: a small but excellent shoulder of mutton, a capon, and four partridges. These alone I bought at market; my little estate here supplied the rest.

Timothy. I behold an Epicurean, nay a Sybaritic, luncheon.

Eusebius. Oh, no, scarcely Carmelitic. But take it in good part, such as it is. My intentions are good even if the feast isn't sumptuous.

Timothy. So far from silent is your house that not only the walls but the cup too says something.

Eusebius. What does it tell you?

Timothy. "No one is harmed but by himself."

Eusebius. The cup speaks in defense of wine, for most people blame the wine when they get a fever or headache from drinking, although they themselves have invited the trouble by drinking too much.

Sophronius. Mine speaks Greek: "In wine there's truth."

Eusebius. A warning that it's not safe for priests or servants of kings to be fond of wine, because wine commonly brings to the tip of a man's tongue whatever he was hiding in his heart.

Sophronius. Among the Egyptians, priests were forbidden to drink wine, even though men were not yet in the habit of committing secrets to them.

Eusebius. Everyone's allowed to drink wine nowadays. Whether or not this is wise, I don't know. Eulalius, what's that little book you are taking from your pocket? It looks very fine, for even on the outside it's all gilded.

Eulalius. But it's more than precious on the inside. These are Paul's letters, which I always carry with me as my favorite delights. I take them out now because your remark reminded me of a certain passage that has puzzled me a good long while, nor have I made up my mind about it even yet. It's in I Corinthians, 6: "All things are lawful unto me, but all things are not expedient: all things are lawful for me, but I will not be brought under the power of any." In the first place, if we believe the Stoics, nothing is useful unless likewise honorable. How, then, does Paul distinguish the lawful from the expedient? Surely whoring or drunkenness is not lawful; therefore how are "all things" lawful? But if Paul is talking about a particular class of things, all of which he would allow, I can't well conjecture from the tone of *this* passage what that class

might be. What immediately follows suggests that he is talking about the choice of foods. For some persons abstained from
meat offered to idols, some from foods forbidden by Moses.
And of meats offered to idols he treats in Chapter 8 and again
in Chapter 10. As though to explain the meaning of this
passage,[29] he says: "All things are lawful for me, but all things
are not expedient: all things are lawful for me, but all
things edify not. Let no man seek his own, but every man
another's wealth. Whatsoever is sold in the shambles, that
eat." [30] What Paul subjoins here seems to agree with what he
had said above: "Meats for the belly, and the belly for meats:
but God shall destroy both it and them." [31] That here too he
had in mind the Jewish choice of foods is indicated by the
close of Chapter 10: "Give none offense, neither to the Jews,
nor to the Gentiles, nor to the Church of God: Even as I
please all men in all things, not seeking mine own profit, but
the profit of many, that they may be saved." "Gentiles" seems
to be connected with meat offered to idols; "Jews" with the
choice of foods; "the Church of God" with the weak of both
races. It was permissible, therefore, to eat anything one liked,
and "to the pure all things are pure." But this may be in-
expedient. That all things were permissible was a matter of
gospel liberty; but charity everywhere regards what contributes to the salvation of our neighbor, and on that account
frequently abstains from what is permitted, preferring to
yield to the welfare of a neighbor rather than exercise its
liberty.[32]

But here a double objection bothers me. First, in the con-
text of the discourse nothing that precedes or follows fits this
sense. For he rebukes the Corinthians for being unruly and
impure by reason of whoring, adultery, and even incest, and

---

[29] I.e., the one in Ch. 6.

[30] I Corinthians 10:23-25.

[31] I Corinthians 6:13.

[32] The Sorbonne condemned the last part of this paragraph (*Opera
Omnia,* Leiden edition, IX, 935B-D).

for going to law "before the unjust." [33] How does "All things are lawful for me, but all things are not expedient" agree with these words? And in what follows he returns to the cause of their shamelessness (he had resumed this earlier, also), dropping the subject of lawsuits. "The body," he says, "is not for fornication, but for the Lord, and the Lord for the body." [34] Yet this objection I can manage to overcome, too, because a little earlier in his list of sins he had mentioned idolatry: "Be not deceived: neither fornicators, nor idolaters, nor adulterers. . . ." [35] Moreover, the eating of meats offered to idols bordered on idolatry. And therefore he adds immediately: "Meats for the belly, and the belly for meats," [36] signifying that for the body's needs one may, for the time being, eat anything he likes unless deterred by compassion for his neighbor. But shamelessness is to be abhorred always and everywhere. Eating is necessary, but the necessity will be taken away at the resurrection of the dead; lusting is wickedness.

But a second difficulty I can't solve: how "But I will not be brought under the power of any" [37] agrees with this passage. For he says he has all things in his power, yet will not be brought under the power of any. If one who abstains lest he give offense is said to be in the power of another, that's just what he says of himself in Chapter 9: "Though I be free from all men, yet have I made myself servant unto all that I might gain all." [38] St. Ambrose,[39] evidently troubled by this difficulty, thinks rather that the Apostle here prepares the way for what in Chapter 9 he says he has the *power* of doing, and what others, either apostles or false apostles, *were* doing—i.e., getting his livelihood from those to whom he preached the gospel.

[33] I Corinthians 6:1.

[34] I Corinthians 6:13.

[35] I Corinthians 6:9.

[36] I Corinthians 6:13.

[37] I Corinthians 6:12.

[38] I Corinthians 9:19. "Gain all" should be "gain the more."

[39] "Commentary on I Corinthians," in Migne, *Patrologia Latina*, XVII, 225C-D.

But although he had a right to do this, he held back, in order to make matters easier for the Corinthians, whom he was rebuking for so many and such egregious sins. Furthermore, whoever accepts anything comes more or less under obligation to the one from whom he accepts it, and loses some of his authority, since he is less free to criticize, and usually the giver won't tolerate criticism by the beneficiary. In this respect, therefore, Paul refrained from what was permissible, to preserve his Apostolic freedom; he wanted to avoid giving offense on this ground, in order that he might denounce their sins more freely and with greater authority. To me Ambrose's notion is not unattractive. If one prefers, nevertheless, to apply this passage to foods, my view is that Paul's "But I will not be brought under the power of any" can be understood thus: "Although, for the sake of my neighbor's salvation and the advancement of the gospel, I abstain sometimes from foods used in sacrifices, or forbidden by the Mosaic law, yet my mind is free, knowing I may eat whatever I please to suit my mere body's needs." But false apostles argued that some foods were unclean in themselves, not to be shunned only on occasion but always, as though they were naturally harmful, just as we refrain from murder and adultery. Those who believed this were "brought under the power" of another, and cut off from the freedom of the gospel. Only Theophylact,[40] as I recall, dissents from all these interpretations: "It is permissible to eat any foods whatever, but not intemperately, for excess produces shamelessness." Although this is sound sense, still it does not seem to me the real meaning of the passage.

I've shown you what perplexes me. It will be left to your kindness to get me out of my difficulties.

Eusebius. Indeed you answer to your name very well. One who can put questions thus doesn't need someone else to answer them. You've expressed your doubt in such a way that I myself am in doubt no longer, even though Paul, since he decided to deal with many matters at the same time, often

[40] "Commentary on I Corinthians," in Migne, *Patrologia Graeca*, CXXIV, 633A-B.

shifts in this letter from one subject to another, and then resumes what he had interrupted.

Chrysoglottus. If I weren't afraid my chatter would interfere with your eating, and if I thought it lawful to mix anything from profane writers with such religious conversation, I'd present something that didn't puzzle but delighted me extremely as I was reading it today.

Eusebius. On the contrary, whatever is devout and contributes to good morals should not be called profane. Of course Sacred Scripture is the basic authority in everything; yet I sometimes run across ancient sayings or pagan writings— even the poets'—so purely and reverently expressed, and so inspired, that I can't help believing their authors' hearts were moved by some divine power. And perhaps the spirit of Christ is more widespread than we understand, and the company of saints includes many not in our calendar. Speaking frankly among friends, I can't read Cicero's *De senectute, De amicitia, De officiis, De Tusculanis quaestionibus* without sometimes kissing the book and blessing that pure heart, divinely inspired as it was. But when, on the other hand, I read these modern writers on government, economics, or ethics—good Lord, how tame they are by comparison! And what lack of feeling they seem to have for what they write! So that I would much rather let all of Scotus and others of his sort perish, than the books of a single Cicero or Plutarch. Not that I condemn the former entirely, but I perceive I am helped by reading the others, whereas I rise from the reading of these somehow less enthusiastic about true virtue, but more disputatious. So don't hesitate to present it, whatever it is.

Chrysoglottus. While most of Tully's books on philosophy seem to breathe something of divinity, I consider the one on old age, written when he himself was old, his swan song, as the Greek proverb puts it. Today I reread it, and learned the following words by heart, since they pleased me most of all: "But if some god granted me power to change my old age and be a child again and cry in the cradle, I should steadfastly refuse; nor, after finishing the course, as it were, should I

like to be called back to the starting point. For what satis-
faction does this life have? Rather, what hardship does it not
have? But should it not have that for certain, undeniably it
has wearisomeness and vexation. I do not wish to complain of
life, as many men, and learned ones too, have often done. Nor
am I sorry to have lived, since I have so lived that I do not
think I was born in vain. And yet I depart from this life as
from an inn, not a home. Nature gave us a lodging to stop at,
not to settle down in. O glorious day when I shall join that
company of souls and leave this tumult and contagion!" [41]
Thus far Cato. What could a Christian have said more
reverently? I wish the conversations of monks, or those of
monks and nuns, were all like this talk of an old pagan with
young pagans.

Eusebius. But someone will object that Cicero's discourse
is a fiction.

Chrysoglottus. To me it matters little whether the credit
belongs to Cato for thinking and uttering such sentiments, or
to Cicero, whose mind by the power of imagination laid hold
upon such divine ideas, and whose pen described these choice
themes with corresponding eloquence. Though I believe that
even if he didn't utter those very words, Cato nevertheless was
in the habit of saying things like them in conversation. Tully
was not so impudent as to depict Cato as other than he really
was, nor, in his dialogue, to overlook decorum—an essential
requirement in this kind of composition, especially when remembrance of that man was fresh in the minds of the writer's
contemporaries.

Theophilus. Very likely, but I'll tell you what came to
mind while you were reciting. I've often wondered at the fact
that although everybody hopes for a long life and dreads
death, I've found scarcely anyone—I don't mean a very aged
man but one beginning to get along in years—who was so
happy that he wouldn't agree with Cato if asked whether he
would be a child again if he could, experiencing all the good
and evil that had already fallen to his lot in life; especially if

41 *De senectute*, xxiii, 83-84.

he called to mind whatever had happened to him for better or worse. Recollection of pleasant things is often accompanied by shame or a bad conscience, so that the mind shrinks from recalling them no less than it shrinks from recalling sorrows. The wisest poets have pointed this out to us, I believe. According to them, it is only after souls have drunk large draughts of forgetfulness from the river Lethe that they are at last enthralled by desire for the bodies they left behind.

Uranius. This is curious, to be sure, and I've often observed examples of it myself. Yet what pleased me rather was "Nor am I sorry to have lived." Now, how many Christians live soberly enough to be able to apply this old man's statements to themselves? Most think they have not lived in vain if, at death, they can leave a large estate got by hook or crook. But Cato's reason for thinking he had not lived in vain was that he had been an honest, upright citizen of the republic and an incorruptible magistrate, and that he left to posterity monuments of his virtue and industry. What could be said more divinely than his "I depart as from an inn, not from a home"? One may use an inn for a while, until the host tells him to go. From his own home one is not easily driven out. And yet it often happens that a collapse or a fire or some other accident forces him out; or even if none of these should occur, the building's crumbling with age warns him to move.

Nephalius. No less choice is the speech of Socrates in Plato: "The human soul is placed in this body as if in a garrison which it must not abandon except by the commander's order, or remain in longer than suits him who stationed it there." [42] The more significant that Plato said "garrison" instead of "house," since we only inhabit a house; in a garrison we are assigned some duty by our commander. Nor is this out of keeping with our Scriptures, which tell us human life is sometimes a warfare, sometimes a battle.

Uranius. Cato's language, I think, agrees admirably with that of Paul,[43] who, writing to the Corinthians, calls the

[42] Cf. *Phaedo,* 62b.
[43] II Corinthians 5:1-2.

heavenly mansion we look for after this life οἰκία and
οἰκητήριον, that is, a home or dwelling. But this poor body he
calls a tabernacle, Greek σκῆνος. "For we that are in this
tabernacle," he says, "do groan, being burdened." [44]

Nephalius. Neither is it out of keeping with the language
of Peter: "I think it meet," he says, "as long as I am in this
tabernacle, to stir you up by putting you in remembrance,
knowing that shortly I must put off this my tabernacle." [45]
What else does Christ proclaim to us than that we should
live and watch as though we were shortly to die, to exert ourselves in good deeds as though we were to live forever? When
we hear that "O glorious day" don't we seem to hear Paul
himself saying, "I desire to depart and to be with Christ"? [46]

Chrysoglottus. How fortunate are they who await death
in such a spirit! But in Cato's speech, splendid though it is,
one might object to the self-confidence as expressive of an
arrogance that ought to be very far from a Christian. Hence I
think I've never read anything in pagan writers more proper
to a true Christian than what Socrates spoke to Crito [47] shortly
before drinking the hemlock: "Whether God will approve of
my works," he said, "I know not; certainly I have tried hard
to please him. Yet I have good hope that he will accept my
efforts." Diffident as he was about his own deeds, yet by reason
of his earnest desire to obey the divine will he conceived a
strong hope that God in his goodness would accept them, because he had endeavored to live righteously.

Nephalius. An admirable spirit, surely, in one who had
not known Christ and the Sacred Scriptures. And so, when I
read such things of such men, I can hardly help exclaiming,
"Saint Socrates, pray for us!"

Chrysoglottus. As for me, there are many times when I do
not hesitate to hope confidently that the souls of Virgil and
Horace are sanctified.

[44] II Corinthians 5:4.
[45] II Peter 1:13-14.
[46] Philippians 1:23.
[47] To Simmias and Cebes, rather: *Phaedo*, 69d.

Nephalius. Yet how many Christians have I seen die ever so bitterly! Some put their trust in what should not be trusted; some, because of bad conscience about their sins, and because of stumbling blocks that certain ignorant persons place in the way of the dying, expire in almost hopeless despair.[48]

Chrysoglottus. No wonder those who have puzzled their heads so much over ceremonies all their lives should die thus.[49]

Nephalius. What do you mean by that word "ceremonies"?

Chrysoglottus. I'll tell you, but let me begin by making very plain that I don't condemn the rites and sacraments of the Church; on the contrary I most emphatically approve of them. I do condemn certain unprincipled or superstitious or (to put it as mildly as I can) simple and uninformed men who teach the people to put their trust in these things, when those that make us truly Christians are neglected.

Nephalius. I don't follow you very well.

Chrysoglottus. I'll try to make it clear. If you look at the majority of Christians, isn't it true that their main reliance in life is in ceremonies? How scrupulously are the ancient rites of the Church performed in baptism! The infant waits outside the church door; exorcism and catechism are carried out; vows taken; Satan abjured with all his pomps and vanities; finally the babe is anointed with oil, marked with the sign of the cross, salted, and dipped; sponsors are given the charge of training the child; upon payment of a sum of money they are released. And now at last the boy is called a Christian—and is one after a fashion. Soon he is anointed again; finally he learns to confess; takes Communion; becomes accustomed to keeping quiet on holy days, to hearing divine service, to fasting at times, to abstaining from meat. And if he does these things, he is considered a Christian beyond question. He marries, and receives another sacrament. He takes orders, and is once more

48 See the colloquy "The Funeral."

49 This remark and the one a few lines later, "their main reliance in life is in ceremonies," offended the Sorbonne (*Opera Omnia,* Leiden edition, IX, 935D-936C).

anointed and consecrated; his clothes are changed; prayers said. All this I approve of, but their doing it from custom rather than from conviction I don't approve of. The notion that nothing else is needed for Christianity I reject absolutely, since a great part of mankind, while trusting to these things, loses no time in making money by hook or crook and becoming enslaved to anger, lust, gluttony, ambition until at last they come to death's door. Here again ceremonies are ready. Confession is made over and over; extreme unction added; the Eucharist administered; sacred candles, a crucifix, holy water are at hand; indulgences produced; a papal brief displayed or bought on the spot for the dying man; a lavish funeral ordered; once again a solemn contract is made; one man shouts in the dying person's ear—sometimes, in fact, pesters him to an earlier death if (as frequently happens) he's loud or well liquored. Although these ceremonies, especially the ones sanctioned by ecclesiastical usage, are acceptable, yet there are also other, more interior, means of helping us to depart from this life with cheerfulness and Christian trust.

Eusebius. You preach piously and truly, to be sure, but meanwhile nobody touches the food. Let no one deceive himself: I told you beforehand to expect nothing beyond a second course, and that a country one, lest anyone promise himself pheasants or woodcocks or Attic delicacies. Remove these things, boy; and serve the rest. You see my horn of penury, not plenty. This is the produce of the little gardens you saw. Don't hold back if there's something you like.

Timothy. There's such variety that the very sight of it refreshes us.

Eusebius. But—that you may not altogether scorn my frugality—this dish would have overjoyed that good Christian monk Hilarion and a hundred of his companions among the monks of that age. For Paul and Anthony, indeed, it would have been a month's provision.[50]

[50] Hilarion, Paul, Anthony: famous early Christian hermits. Anthony was the reputed founder of monasticism.

Timothy. Nor would Peter, Prince of Apostles, have despised it, I believe, when he dwelt with Simon the tanner.[51]

Eusebius. Nor Paul either, in my opinion, when need compelled him to work at night as a tentmaker.[52]

Timothy. We owe this to God's goodness. But I would rather go hungry with Peter and Paul, provided the lack of bodily nourishment were compensated by spiritual delights.

Eusebius. Rather let us learn from Paul both to abound and to suffer hunger. When there is lack, let us thank Jesus Christ for supplying us with means of self-control and patience; when there is plenty, we should thank the generosity of him who freely invites us and rouses us to love of him. Enjoying in moderation what the divine goodness has provided, we ought to be mindful of the poor—who by God's will are without that in which we abound—in order that there may be occasion of mutual goodness by each to the other. Since we are granted enough to enable us to relieve brotherly need, we may win God's mercy; and the poor, restored by our generosity, thank God for our good will and commend us to him in their prayers.

And well does this come to mind. Here, boy, tell my wife to send what's left of the roast to our Gudula. She's a neighbor who's pregnant and poor, but blessed in spirit. Her husband, an idle spendthrift, died recently, leaving her nothing but a pack of children.

Timothy. Christ commanded us to give to everyone who asks. If I did that, I'd have to beg myself within a month.

Eusebius. I believe Christ means those who ask for necessities. Those who seek, nay demand, or rather extort, large sums to make Lucullan feasts or—worse yet—to cater to their gluttony and lust, it is charity to refuse. More than that, it's robbery to bestow on those who will use it ill what ought to have relieved the instant distress of our neighbors. Hence those who adorn monasteries or churches at excessive cost,

[51] Acts 9:43, 10:6.
[52] Acts 18:3.

when meanwhile so many of Christ's living temples are in
danger of starving, shiver in their nakedness, and are tortured
by want of necessities, seem to me almost guilty of a capital
crime.[53] When I was in Britain I saw St. Thomas' tomb
laden with innumerable precious jewels in addition to other
incredible riches.[54] I'd rather have this superfluous wealth
spent on the poor than kept for the use of officials who will
plunder it all sooner or later. I'd decorate the tomb with
branches and flowers; this, I think, would be more pleasing to
the saint. In Italy I saw a certain Carthusian monastery, not
far from Pavia. In it is a church built of white marble within
and without, from top to bottom; and almost everything inside—altars, columns, tombs—is marble. What was the good of
pouring out so much money to enable a few lone monks to
sing in a marble church which even to them is a burden, not
a benefit, because it's constantly overrun with visitors who col-
lect there merely to see that marble church?

There I learned of something still more foolish: that they
have a legacy of three thousand ducats a year to spend on
building. And some people think it a crime to divert that
money, contrary to the testator's intentions, to pious uses.
They prefer to pull down what they begin rather than not to
build at all. Since these facts are notorious, I thought I should
mention them, although our own churches furnish a great
many similar examples from time to time. This strikes me as
a thirst for glory, not charity. Rich men covet a monument
for themselves in churches where formerly there was not room
for saints.[55] They take care to have their likenesses carved and
painted, with their names and an inscription about their gift
added. And with these things they fill up a large part of the
church. The time will come, I suppose, when they'll insist on
being buried on the very altars.

Someone will ask, "Do you think their liberality should

[53] This passage, too, gave offense to the Sorbonne (*Opera Omnia*,
Leiden edition, IX, 936C-E).
[54] See "A Pilgrimage for Religion's Sake."
[55] See "The Funeral."

be refused?" By no means, if what they offer is worthy of the temple of God. But if I were a priest or a bishop, I would urge upon those thickheaded courtiers or merchants that if they wanted to have their sins forgiven in God's sight, they should spend their money secretly, for the support of those who really need it. They consider money wasted that is scattered thus, anonymously and in small amounts, to relieve the immediate needs of the poor—no memorial of it might survive for posterity! For my part, I think no money is better spent than that for which Christ himself will be most assuredly our debtor.

Timothy. Don't you think what is given to monasteries well spent?

Eusebius. I'd give them something if I were rich, but I'd give for their need, not their magnificence, and to those in which I perceived a zeal for true religion to flourish.

Timothy. Many think what is given to public beggars is not well spent.

Eusebius. Something should be given to those, too, at times, yet with discrimination. I should think it wise for each city to look after its own, and not to tolerate vagabonds wandering about hither and yon—particularly the able-bodied ones, who, I imagine, need a job rather than a dole.

Timothy. Then to whom do you think we should give chiefly? How much, and to what extent?

Eusebius. That would be very hard to define precisely. In the first place, there ought to be a will to assist everybody. Next, so far as my slender means permit, I give whenever occasion presents itself, especially to those whose poverty and honesty are known to me. And if I haven't the means, I urge others to be generous.

Timothy. But do you permit us to speak freely here in your kingdom?

Eusebius. Oh, yes, more frankly than in your own home.

Timothy. You disapprove of spending too much on churches, and yet you could have built this house for much less.

Eusebius. Well, I think it's in the modest class. Or call it elegant if you prefer; certainly it's not luxurious, unless I'm mistaken. Mendicants build more splendidly. Yet these gardens of mine, such as they are, pay tax to the needy; and every day I economize in something and deny myself and my family in order to be more bountiful toward the poor.

Timothy. If everyone were of your mind, a great many now suffering undeserved poverty would be better off; and on the other hand, there wouldn't be so many of those stout people who deserve to learn the sobriety and restraint that necessity could teach them.

Eusebius. Maybe so, but shouldn't we season this flat dessert with something sweet?

Timothy. We've had more than enough sweets.

Eusebius. But I'll bring out what you won't dislike even if you're full.

Timothy. What's that?

Eusebius. A codex of the Gospels, which, since it's my most splendid possession, I'll fetch to crown the feast. Read, boy, from the place where you stopped.

Boy. "No man can serve two masters: for either he will hate the one, and love the other; or else he will hold to the one, and despise the other. Ye cannot serve God and mammon. Therefore I say unto you, Take no thought for your life, what ye shall eat . . . nor yet for your body, what ye shall put on. Is not the life more than meat, and the body than raiment?" [56]

Eusebius. Hand me the book. In this passage Jesus Christ seems to me to have said the same thing twice, because in place of what he said first, "will hate," he immediately puts "will despise"; and for "will love," "will hold to": the meaning is the same with the persons changed.

Timothy. I don't quite follow.

Eusebius. Then let's demonstrate it mathematically, if you like. In the earlier part put A for one, B for the other; again, in the latter, put B for the one, A for the other, in re-

[56] Matthew 6:24-25.

verse order. For either he will hate A and love B, or will hold to B and despise A. Isn't it plain that A is twice hated and B twice loved?

Timothy. Very clear.

Eusebius. But this conjunction "or," especially when repeated, indicates a contrary or certainly a different meaning. Otherwise wouldn't it be absurd to say, "Either Peter will defeat me and I'll yield, or I'll yield and Peter will defeat me"?

Timothy. A nice sophism, God help me!

Eusebius. It will seem nice to me, too, in the end, if you solve it for me.

Theophilus. My mind dreams and delivers something, I know not what. If you order me to, I'll bring it forth before you, whatever it is, and you'll be the interpreters or midwives.

Eusebius. Although it's commonly considered unlucky to recall dreams at a feast, and hardly decent to be in labor in the presence of so many men, nevertheless we'll be glad to receive your dream, or, if you prefer, the offspring of your mind.

Theophilus. In this utterance the action rather than the person is shifted, it seems to me. And this expression, "one, and . . . one . . ." is not related to A and B, but each part of the expression refers to either "one." Whichever "one" you choose is now opposed to what is indicated by the other. As if you should say, "Either you will exclude A and admit B, or admit A and exclude B." You observe here that although the person remains, the action is changed, and this is so said of A that it makes no difference if you should say the same of B, in this way: "Either you will exclude B and admit A, or admit B and exclude A."

Eusebius. You've explained the problem to us very acutely indeed, nor could any mathematician have demonstrated it better in the sand.

Sophronius. I'm more puzzled by the part forbidding us to worry about the morrow,[57] since Paul himself worked with his hands to get his living,[58] severely rebuking lazy folk and

57 Matthew 6:34.
58 Acts 18:3; II Thessalonians 3:8.

those who are glad to live off others. He warns them to work [59]
and tells them manual labor is good for them, because it enables them to help the needy. Isn't the labor by which a poor
husband supports his beloved wife and dear children pious
and sanctified?

Timothy. In my judgment, that question can be answered
in different ways. First, as relates particularly to those times.
The Apostles, who traveled far and wide for the sake of
preaching the gospel, had to be relieved of the worry of getting a living. They had no time to earn their bread by manual labor, especially when they knew no craft but fishing.
Now times have changed, and we all have leisure enough;
we're just lazy. A second solution is this: Christ did not forbid labor but anxiety. And by anxiety he meant the common
feeling of men who are concerned above all else with making
a living; everything else neglected, they attend to this alone,
devoted to this single care. The Lord himself virtually declares this when he denies that the same man can serve two
masters, since "serving" means "completely devoted to." Therefore he wants the first and foremost care—not the *sole* care—
to be that of spreading the gospel. For he says, "Seek ye first the
kingdom of God, and all these things shall be added unto
you." [60] He does not say "seek only" but "seek first." But "the
morrow" is an intentional exaggeration, I think, for he means
the distant future. Those whose hearts are set on this world
habitually worry about the future and try to prepare for it.

Eusebius. We accept your interpretation. But what does
he mean by saying "Take no thought for your life,[61] what ye
shall eat"? [62] The body wears clothing, but the soul doesn't
eat.

Timothy. Here he calls the soul life, I think. The soul is
endangered if you take away food, but not if you strip off
clothing, which is for modesty rather than necessity. If a per-

[59] II Thessalonians 3:11; I Thessalonians 4:11-12.
[60] Matthew 6:33; Luke 12:31.
[61] *Animae* (Vulgate).
[62] Matthew 6:25, 31.

son is perforce naked, he doesn't die instantly. But starvation is death for sure.

Eusebius. I don't quite see the connection between this statement and what follows: "Is not the life more than meat, and the body than raiment?" For if life is of great value, we should be the more zealous to preserve it.

Timothy. This argument does not dispel our uncertainty but adds to it.

Eusebius. But you misinterpret Christ's meaning. By this argument he increases our trust in the Father. If the benevolent Father gave freely and of his own accord what is more precious, He will likewise add what is more common. He who gave the soul will not deny food; He who gave the body will add clothing from somewhere. Relying on his kindness, therefore, we have no reason to be distracted by anxiety over minor matters. What remains, then, except to turn our whole care and zeal to the love of heavenly things, using this world as though we used it not; and, utterly rejecting earthly riches, together with Satan and all his wiles, with a whole and fervent heart serve God alone, who will not forsake his children.

But meanwhile nobody is touching the dessert. Surely it's permissible to enjoy this, which is produced for us at home with no trouble at all.

Timothy. Our bodies have had quite enough.

Eusebius. Your minds too, I trust.

Timothy. Our minds have fed even more richly.

Eusebius. Then remove these things, boy, and bring the basin. Let us wash, my friends, in order that, cleansed of any fault we may have committed at this feast, we may sing a hymn to God. I'll finish the one I began from Chrysostom, if you like.

Timothy. Please do.

Eusebius. "Glory to thee, O Lord; glory to thee, O thou holy one; glory to thee, O king. As now thou hast given us meat, fill us with joy and gladness in the Holy Spirit, that we may be found acceptable in thy sight, nor be shamed when thou renderest to each according to his works."

Boy. Amen.

Timothy. A devout and beautiful hymn, without question.

Eusebius. St. Chrysostom does not disdain to interpret it, too.

Timothy. Where?

Eusebius. In his fifty-sixth [63] homily on Matthew.

Timothy. I'll read it without fail this very day. But there's one thing, meantime, I want to learn from you: why do we pray for Christ's glory three times, and by the triple title of "lord," "holy one," and "king"?

Eusebius. Because all glory belongs to him, but especially ought we to praise him by the triple name. First, because by his sacred blood he released us from the devil's tyranny and claimed us as his own; whence we call him lord. Next, because, not content with having freely pardoned all our sins by his spirit, he bestowed his righteousness upon us, that we might seek after holiness. And for this reason we call him holy, because he is the sanctifier of all men. Finally, because from him we hope for the reward of the heavenly kingdom, where he now sits at the right hand of God the Father; hence we call him king. And all this blessedness we owe to his grace, freely granted us: that instead of having the devil as master, or tyrant rather, we have Jesus Christ for lord; instead of the dregs and filth of sin we have innocence and holiness; instead of hell the joys of the heavenly life.

Timothy. A truly reverent thought.

Eusebius. Since now this is the first time I've had you to dinner, I won't send you away without presents, but with ones that are in keeping with our style. Ho there, boy, bring my going-away gifts. Draw lots, or choose for yourselves, it makes no difference. They're all worth about the same—nothing, that is. These aren't the lots of Heliogabalus,[64] by which this man wins a hundred horses and that one as many flies.

---

[63] No. 55 in some editions; see note 13.

[64] Roman emperor (A.D. 218-222), infamous for his extravagance and depravity. See *Scriptores Historiae Augustae*, "Antoninus Elagabalus," xxii.

There are four little books, two clocks, a small lamp, and a case with Memphian pens.[65] I think these suit you better than balsam juice or tooth powder or a mirror, if I know you well.

Timothy. They're all so fine that it's hard for us to choose. Distribute them yourself, as you think best; then whatever one gets will be all the more welcome.

Eusebius. This little vellum book contains Solomon's proverbs. It teaches wisdom, and is decorated with gold because gold symbolizes wisdom. This shall be given to our white-haired friend, that, in accordance with evangelical teaching, wisdom be given to him who hath wisdom and he may have abundance.

Timothy. Assuredly I'll endeavor to need it the less.

Eusebius. The clock, imported from far-off Dalmatia (if I may thus praise my own present), will suit Sophronius, for I know how thrifty of time he is, how he won't let any part of that great treasure go without making good use of it.

Sophronius. No, no; you're advising a lazy man to be diligent.

Eusebius. This little book has Matthew's Gospel on vellum: worthy of a jeweled cover were it not that no bookcase or cover is dearer to it than a man's heart. This then for you, learned Theophilus, to make you more like your name.

Theophilus. I'll try to see that you won't regret your gift.

Eusebius. Here are Paul's Epistles, which you, Eulalius, who are always quoting Paul, like to carry about with you. You wouldn't have him in your mouth unless he were in your heart. After this he'll be more readily in your hands and eyes too.

Eulalius. This is to give counsel, not a gift. No gift is more precious than good counsel.

Eusebius. The little oil lamp will suit Chrysoglottus, an insatiable reader and, as Tully [66] says, a mighty devourer of books.

[65] Egyptian, i.e., reed, pens. Cf. Martial, xiv, 38.
[66] *De Finibus,* III, ii, 7.

Chrysoglottus. I thank you twice: first, for an uncommonly nice present; secondly, for admonishing a sleepy fellow to be alert.

Eusebius. The pen case goes by rights to Theodidactus, a most graceful and prolific writer; and I deem these pens to be most fortunate by which the glory of our Lord Jesus Christ will be celebrated, especially by so talented a writer.

Theodidactus. Would that you could furnish the inspiration as you do the instruments!

Eusebius. This codex contains some short works of Plutarch, the *Moralia,* selected and skillfully copied by someone expert in Greek writing. So much piety do I find in them that I think it marvelous such Christian-like notions could have come into a pagan mind. This will be presented to Uranius, a young Hellenist. A clock remains. That's for our Nephalius, who's very frugal of time.

Nephalius. We thank you, not only for your little presents but also for the testimonials. For this is not so much distributing gifts as compliments.

Eusebius. My thanks to you, rather, on two counts: first, for being so good about my simple style of living; secondly, for refreshing my mind with your conversation, which was equally learned and devout. I'll send you away without knowing what sort of time you've had, but undoubtedly I'll take leave of you a better and wiser man myself. I know pipes or jesters aren't to your taste; much less, dice. So, if you like, let's beguile a brief hour by seeing the other wonders of my palace.

Timothy. We were just about to beg that of you.

Eusebius. No need to beg one who promises sincerely. I suppose you've already seen enough of this summer courtyard. It has a triple view, and whichever way you look you're confronted by the most delightful verdure of gardens. With the sliding windows you may, if you like, shut out the weather, should clouds or winds make it a bit disagreeable; and if the heat annoys, you may shut out the sun by closing the thick shutters from the outside and the thin ones from inside. When

I lunch here, I seem to eat in a garden, not a house. For the walls, too, have flowers mingled with their green, and there are rather good pictures. Here Christ celebrates the Last Supper with his chosen disciples. Here Herod observes his birthday with a fatal feast. Here Dives of the Gospel story, shortly to go down to hell, dines sumptuously; Lazarus, soon to be received into Abraham's bosom, is driven from the gates.

Timothy. I don't quite recognize this story.

Eusebius. Cleopatra is trying to outdo Anthony in voluptuousness. She's already swallowed a pearl, and puts out her hand to take another one.[67] Here the Lapithae [68] are fighting. Here Alexander the Great pierces Clitus with a spear.[69] These examples warn us to be temperate at feasts, and deter us from drunkenness and sensuality. Now let's go into the library, which is furnished with choice if not numerous books.

Timothy. Clearly this place is hallowed, so radiant is everything.

Eusebius. Here you see the main part of my wealth. For on the table you saw nothing but glass and pewter. There isn't a silver vessel in the entire house; just one gilded cup, which I treasure out of affection for the person who gave it to me. This hanging globe puts the whole world before your eyes. Here on the walls every region is painted in a larger space. On the other walls you see pictures of famous teachers. To paint them all would have been an endless task. Christ, seated on the mountain with his hand outstretched, has the foremost place. The Father appears above his head, saying "Hear ye him." With spreading wings the Holy Spirit enfolds him in dazzling light.

Timothy. A work worthy of Apelles, so help me.

Eusebius. Adjoining the library is a study, narrow but neat. When the board's removed you see a small hearth to use if you're cold. In summer it seems a solid wall.

---

[67] See Pliny, *Natural History*, IX, lviii, 119-121.

[68] A Thessalian people who fought against the Centaurs (Ovid, *Met.*, xii, 210ff.).

[69] Plutarch, *Alexander*, l-li.

Timothy. To me everything here seems precious. And there's a delightful scent.

Eusebius. I try very hard to keep the house shining and fragrant. To do both is not expensive. The library has its own balcony, overlooking the garden; connected with it is a chapel.

Timothy. A place fit for deity.

Eusebius. Now let's go on to those three galleries above the ones you saw, the ones looking out on the kitchen garden. These upper ones have a view on each side, but through windows that can be closed—especially in these walls that do not look on the inner garden—to make the house safer. Here on the left, because there is more light and the wall has fewer windows, is painted in order the entire life of Jesus as related by the four Evangelists, up to the sending forth of the Holy Spirit and the first preaching of the Apostles from Acts. Place names are added, too, that the spectator may read by which water or on which mountain the event took place; also captions summarizing the whole story, e.g., Jesus' words, "I will: be thou clean." On the opposite side are corresponding figures and prophecies of the Old Testament, particularly from the Prophets and Psalms, which contain nothing other than the life of Christ and the Apostles, told in a different manner. Here I stroll sometimes, conversing with myself and meditating upon that inexpressible purpose of God by which he willed to restore the human race through his son. Sometimes my wife, or some friend pleased by sacred subjects, keeps me company.

Timothy. Who could be bored in this house?

Eusebius. No one who has learned to live with himself. Along the top edge of the paintings are added, as a kind of border, the heads of the popes with their names; opposite, the heads of the Caesars, to help one remember history. In each corner of the wings is a small bedchamber where one can rest and from which one can see the orchard and my little birds. Here in the farthest corner of the meadow you see another small building, where we sometimes dine in summer, and where anyone of the family who is stricken with a contagious disease is cared for.

Timothy. Some people deny that such diseases are to be shunned.

Eusebius. Then why do they shun a pit or poison? Or do they fear this less because they don't see it? Neither do we see the venom of a basilisk, which darts from his eyes. When the situation absolutely requires, I wouldn't hesitate to risk my life. To risk it without reason is reckless folly; to endanger the lives of others is cruelty.

There are some other things, too, that are worth seeing. I'll ask my wife to show them to you. Stay here three whole days, and consider this house your own. Feast your eyes, feast your minds. For I have business elsewhere; I must ride to some neighboring villages.

Timothy. Money matters?

Eusebius. I wouldn't leave such friends for the sake of money.

Timothy. Perhaps there's hunting somewhere.

Eusebius. Hunting, yes, but I'm hunting something other than boars and stags.

Timothy. What, then?

Eusebius. I'll tell you. In one village a certain friend lies critically ill. The doctor fears for his body; I fear for his soul, rather. Since, in my opinion, he is scarcely prepared to depart as befits a Christian, I'm going to be at hand with good counsel, so that he may be helped whether he dies or recovers. In another village a serious difference has arisen between two men; not bad men, certainly, but stubborn ones. If the quarrel should become sharper, I fear it would draw many others into a feud. I'll try my best to bring them to good terms again, for I have bonds of long standing with both. These are my quarry. If my hunting goes as I wish, we'll have a victory celebration here without delay.

Timothy. Good hunting! Our prayer is that Christ, not Delia, may favor you.

Eusebius. I'd rather have this prize than inherit two thousand ducats.

Timothy. Will you return soon?

Eusebius. Not until I've tried everything. Hence I can't name a definite time. Meanwhile enjoy yourselves with my things as with your own, and farewell.

Timothy. May the Lord Jesus prosper your going and coming!